The Prisoners of 1776

Also from Westphalia Press
westphaliapress.org

The Idea of the Digital University

Criminology Confronts Cultural Change

Eight Decades in Syria

Avant-Garde Politician

Socrates: An Oration

Strategies for Online Education

Conflicts in Health Policy

Material History and Ritual Objects

Jiu-Jitsu Combat Tricks

Opportunity and Horatio Alger

Careers in the Face of Challenge

Bookplates of the Kings

Collecting American Presidential Autographs

Misunderstood Children

Original Cables from the Pearl Harbor Attack

Social Satire and the Modern Novel

The Amenities of Book Collecting

Trademark Power

A Definitive Commentary on Bookplates

James Martineau and Rebuilding Theology

Royalty in All Ages

The Middle East: New Order or Disorder?

The Man Who Killed President Garfield

Chinese Nights Entertainments: Stories from Old China

Understanding Art

Homeopathy

The Signpost of Learning

Collecting Old Books

The Boy Chums Cruising in Florida Waters

The Thomas Starr King Dispute

Salt Water Game Fishing

Lariats and Lassos

Mr. Garfield of Ohio

The Wisdom of Thomas Starr King

The French Foreign Legion

War in Syria

Naturism Comes to the United States

Water Resources: Iniatives and Agendas

Designing, Adapting, Strategizing in Online Education

Feeding the Global South

The Design of Life: Development from a Human Perspective

The Prisoners of 1776: A Relic of the Revolution

by Rev. R. Livesey

WESTPHALIA PRESS

An Imprint of Policy Studies Organization

Westphalia Press
An imprint of Policy Studies Organization
1527 New Hampshire Ave., NW
Washington, D.C. 20036
info@ipsonet.org

ISBN-13: 978-1-63391-550-3
ISBN-10: 1-63391-550-6

Cover design by Jeffrey Barnes:
jbarnesbook.design

Daniel Gutierrez-Sandoval, Executive Director
PSO and Westphalia Press

Updated material and comments on this edition
can be found at the Westphalia Press website:
www.westphaliapress.org

COMMODORE JOHN PAUL JONES' FLEET LEAVING L'ORIENT

A RELIC

of the

REVOLUTION.

TO THE SURVIVORS OF THE OLD REVOLUTION THIS LITTLE
VOLUME IS RESPECTFULLY

Dedicated by the Publisher.

1854.

Stereotyped and Printed
By George C. Rand and Company,
No. 3 Cornhill, Boston.

THE PRISONERS OF 1776;

A

RELIC OF THE REVOLUTION.

CONTAINING

A FULL AND PARTICULAR ACCOUNT OF THE SUFFERINGS
AND PRIVATIONS OF ALL THE AMERICAN PRISONERS
CAPTURED ON THE HIGH SEAS, AND CARRIED INTO
PLYMOUTH, ENGLAND, DURING THE

REVOLUTION OF 1776.

ALSO,

AN ACCOUNT OF THE SEVERAL CRUISES OF THE SQUADRON
UNDER THE COMMAND OF

COMMODORE JOHN PAUL JONES,

PRIZES TAKEN, ETC. ETC.

BY

REV. R. LIVESEY.

COMPILED FROM THE JOURNAL OF CHARLES HERBERT, OF NEWBURYPORT,
MASS., WHO WAS TAKEN PRISONER IN THE BRIGANTINE DOLTON,
DEC. 1776, AND CONFINED IN OLD MILL PRISON,
PLYMOUTH, ENGLAND.

BOSTON:

PUBLISHED FOR THE PROPRIETOR, BY

GEO. C. RAND.

1854.

CONTENTS.

CHAPTER IV.

CHAPTER V.

CHAPTER VI.

CHAPTER VII.

CHAPTER VIII.

CHAPTER IX.

CHAPTER X.

CHAPTER XI.

CHAPTER XII.

CHAPTER XIII.

CHAPTER XIV.

CHAPTER XV.

CHAPTER XVI.

CHAPTER XVII.

CHAPTER XVIII.

12 CONTENTS.

PREFACE.

In presenting the following pages to the reader, the publisher has no ambition to aspire to the character of an author, and what is perhaps more rare, he has no private interest to serve; he does not seek to gratify the fastidious part of the community, who would have more respect for the dress, or appearance, than for the subject matter. He is perfectly aware that the Journal is not without some imperfections; but it must be kept in mind that it was not written for the public, with an eye to publication, or to make a book — but simply as a memorandum of the events of each day. Yet when we take into consideration all the circumstances, it is little less than a miracle; consider the author: a youth of scarcely nineteen summers — then the places where the records were made — the cable tier of a man-of-war, the gloomy recesses of a prison, or on board the battle ship, where three or four hundred men were crowded together for the purposes of strife and blood; then take into consideration the prohibition of all materials for writing in prison, the vigilance of the guards, and the frequent

13

search made among the prisoners, and it becomes a matter of surprise, not that it has some imperfections, but that it exists at all, and especially that it was never interrupted. For the long imprisonment of more than *two years*, it seems to have been providentially preserved, for the purposes of bringing to light the hidden things of darkness, that those who should come after may be admonished and instructed.

The reader will find the Journal free from all appearance of *design* or effort; it is perfectly natural; what is seen or heard is recorded with hardly a note or comment, from first to last; through their medium we are conducted through the hold of the prison-ship, and witness the privations and sufferings of the hapless victims; the prison hospital is thrown open to our inspection, not as transient visitors, but as witnesses of the daily occurrences; here we see justice and mercy meeting together; the walls, the bars, the guards, tell that here stern justice holds its victims, while the attendant physician, and gentle patience of the nurse, speak of Mercy's visits, and pity. Then the prison doors grate on their hinges, and we enter; the vacant stare of the sons of Sorrow meet us, while their meager forms, sallow countenances and ragged habiliments, speak of their privations and misery; we seem to listen to their tale of woe, and hear them tell of happy homes and kind friends in their native land; we can almost taste their scanty and uninviting portions, and our sympathies become deeply interested, until we share in all their anxieties to obtain deliverance; we are sometimes almost suffocated while following the

diggers in their excavations, to force a subterranean
passage to the light of day and air of freedom; anon
we are bounding over the fields as the minions of tyran-
ny pursue us, until, weary and exhausted, we feel their
ruthless hands upon us to drag us back to our gloomy
habitations; then we feel the cold chill run over us, as
we look forward to forty days and nights in darkness
and solitude in the "Black hole," on half the usual allowance of ordinary prisoners; we become acquainted
with the "Two Fathers," the messengers of Love and
Pity — and while the donations continue we seem to
enjoy a respite; hope and fear alternately rise and sink,
until the donation closes, and transient joy gives way
to deeper gloom, until some of the less determined seek
relief on board the· enemy's ships of war, where they
will be compelled to meet their friends and countrymen
in the bloody strife — a destiny more horrible to the
mind capable of reflection, than the protracted miseries
of the prison cell.

At length the star of hope rises, and the news of a
cartel is received; now it arrives, and we are straining
our eyes through the dim light of the grated window
to look on the ship, as she lays in the creek.   Post
after post is anxiously looked for until the agent musters
his wretched charge and reads as follows: "His Majesty has been graciously pleased to pardon one hundred
of you, in order to an exchange."   The names of the
hundred are read, while tears of joy point out the happy
ones.   Once more the prison doors give way — and
with what rapture they hail the breath of freedom!

From the time that Mr. Herbert entered the service

of the United States under the command of Commodore Jones, the entries in his journal are less frequent
and less full; still, if it had not been for the unfortunate
loss of several pages of the Journal, it would have
been sufficiently full, to have conducted the reader
through their several cruizes, to their arrival home; as
it is, we have endeavored to fill up the vacuum by extracts from the official reports of Commodore *Paul Jones.*

It is believed that the reader will receive profit and
pleasure from the numerous and various incidents here
related, and from the information imparted on a variety
of subjects, especially as it shows the views and feelings of the people of England on the subject of the
war then raging between this and the mother country;
and that the strong sympathy manifested towards the
prisoners, in the collection of upwards of *thirty thousand dollars* for their relief, together with all the private
donations, not included in the above, will be an everlast-
ing monument to the benevolence of British Christians,
and may tend to soften our prejudices and lead to
stronger sympathies for each other, and greater efforts
to promote each other's welfare, and mutual feelings
of peace and good will.

A list of the prisoners, with the places to which they
belonged, and vessels in which they were taken, also a
notice of such as had made their escape, had died, or
entered the service of Great Britain, will no doubt be
acceptable to such as had friends in the service of their
country, and of whom, perhaps, they have never since
heard.   The list was taken, as will be seen, a short
time before Mr. Herbert left prison.

The indulgence of the critic is hoped for, under the assurance that the task of preparing the Journal for the press has been arduous, as much of it was originally written in figures to secure secrecy, and had to be spelled out by reference to the key; that the task was performed amidst a press of more important duties, and with a fixed purpose of devoting all the avails of the sales of the work to the widow of the author, after paying the expense of publication.

SKETCH OF THE AUTHOR.

It is perfectly natural to expect, in presenting any work to the public, and more especially of the nature of a journal, that the reader will desire to know something of the character of its author, in order to determine what degree of confidence the writer is entitled to, — whether the statements made are to be depended upon or not. In compliance with this reasonable demand, we will endeavor to impart such information as we possess, believing that it will be perfectly satisfactory.

Charles Herbert was the son of John Herbert, of Newburyport, Mass. His mother's name was Jane, daughter of Colonel Pierce of that town. Mr. Charles Herbert was born November 17th, in the year of our Lord 1757, but, being deprived of his mother by death, at the early age of two months, he was committed to the care of a maiden aunt — Miss Lydia Pierce, sister of his mother. The influence of early training, as developed in the life of Mr. Herbert, is very creditable to his early tutoress. Moral and religious principle must

18

have taken a deep root in his young heart, to have preserved that heart from the gross and corrupting influence of the society into which he was afterwards thrown. The fruit appears in lovely contrast with the abandoned profligacy of many of his companions, and no doubt afforded him abundant consolation in the hours of suffering and solitude. His character gave to him a sort of pre-eminence among his fellows, and an influence with his captors and keepers, which his companions did not share. He was a true patriot; neither frowns nor flatteries could move him to abandon his country's interest. If good tidings reach him, his heart exults with joy; if dark clouds hang over the prospects of the patriot band, he is sorrowful, and will not be comforted; he can endure hunger, confinement, or reproach — any thing but the extinguishing of his country's hope. Others, for the sake of personal liberty, can join the standard of the enemy: but not so with him; he cannot betray the cause of his country, or go to battle against *his brother*.

From the Journal the reader will learn that Mr. Herbert entered on board the Dolton, Nov. 15, 1776, being less than nineteen years of age, and returned to Newburyport Aug. 23, 1780, having been absent nearly four years, two of which he spent as a prisoner, in a foreign land. The sufferings of this period were of the most distressing kind — hunger, cold, sickness, and privation. After his release, by an exchange of prisoners, brought about by the efforts of Dr. Franklin, then Minister to France, Mr. Herbert joined the Alliance frigate, commanded by Captain Landais, forming part of the squadron of Commodore J. Paul Jones. He was one of those sent to Bergen, in Norway, then a part of the kingdom of Denmark, with prizes — which prizes were seized by the Danish government and delivered to the English Consul, which forms the basis of the "Denmark Claims," so called; and which amounted then, according to Dr. Franklin, to at least fifty thousand pounds sterling. The crews of these vessels, on their return from Denmark, were kindly entertained by Dr. Franklin, at his house; and on leaving, he paid their expenses and gave each person a crown. Mr. Herbert preserved his, as a sacred treasure, as long as he lived, but it has since his death been lost. It is to be hoped that those claims against Denmark will be brought to a speedy settlement, and the few survivors of the eventful scenes of Paul Jones' career be rewarded for their sufferings. Mr. Herbert possessed a remarkably active mind, prompt and ready on all occasions; he met every emergency with the utmost self-possession. This is seen in his conduct when the brig was taken, and after he became a prisoner. He could be carpenter, carver, shoemaker, merchant, could make boxes, sell tobacco, or labor in any way to make a shift, to prevent starvation. Nor did he neglect his mind; he bought several books at extravagant prices, which he read, and loaned to his fellow prisoners. Among other studies perused in prison he became master of *navigation*. His journal, which is a standing monument of his genius and industry, was concealed, while writing, in his boots, and as each page became full, it was conveyed to a chest with a double bottom, and there secreted until he left prison.

It is probable the existence of the journal was known to very few, if any, in prison, as the most serious consequences must have followed its discovery. How often in the silent hours of midnight, by the light made from the marrow of a bone, did he trace the record of each eventful day? It has never been known that any journal of any length of time was kept by any other person: it is believed none exists; and to the friends of those who were taken by the enemy and died in prison, or escaped but have not been heard from, or who went on board English men-of-war, "to serve, and continue to serve in his Majesty's service," the journal of Mr. Herbert must be of great interest and satisfaction. After Mr. Herbert's return to Newburyport, Aug. 23, 1780, we have no account of his being employed in the service of his country, other than as a private citizen; indeed, his constitution had received so severe a shock by his long imprisonment and great exposure, that his health was much enfeebled. He soon entered into business as a block-maker, and on the 8th of November, 1783, was united in marriage to Miss *Molly Butler*, by Rev. John Murray, of Newburyport. He continued in the business of block-maker until his death, which occurred on the 4th of September, A. D. 1808. Mr. Herbert had one brother, who died in the morning of life, by a fall occasioned by moving some freight belonging to him on board a vessel. Mrs. Herbert became the mother of fourteen children, six of whom are still living. She is still, at the advanced age of eighty-four, lingering among us as a relic of a people precious in our memory; and should there be a surplus after paying the expenses of publishing this work, if still living, she will enjoy a liberal share thereof.

It is to be regretted that Mrs. Herbert has not been able to obtain either the pension allowed by the law of our land to widows of Revolutionary soldiers and sailors, or the prize money due to her husband from government. How slow are we to reward those who struggled hard for our liberties.

The above facts might be confirmed by the testimony of some of our most distinguished citizens, if necessary.

Hoping that liberal sales will enable the publisher to render to the widow of Charles Herbert a liberal donation, it is submitted to a generous public, by the publisher.   R. LIVESEY.

Boston, July, 1847.

RELIC OF THE REVOLUTION.

CHAPTER I.

The Dolton sailed — Was taken — Breach of Honor — Treatment, &c. — Disagreeable Lodgings — Advantage of being small — A Report — English Women — Royal Salute — Removed — A Prize brought in — Daily Allowance on board His Majesty's Ships — The Charming Sally — Orders.

THE brig DOLTON sailed from Newburyport, November 15th, 1776, and from Portsmouth, on the 26th of the same month, and on the 24th of December following, about nine o'clock in the evening, we were taken by the *Reasonable*, man-of-war, of sixty-four guns.   As her cruise was over, she was bound to Plymouth, England.   The first lieutenant of the ship was the first man that boarded us, and he ordered us all on board the ship as fast as the boats could carry us, and would give us no time to collect our clothes, promising us, however, upon his word and honor, that we

23

should have them all sent on board the next day.
Some of our company trusted to this assurance,
but I thought it not best to do the like. I was
stationed upon the main-top when we were taken,
and had not so good an opportunity to save my
clothes, as those below ; yet I saved more than
any of the foremast hands; for as soon as I found
that we were taken, I made all speed from the top
down to my chest. I broke it open and shifted
myself from head to foot — putting on two shirts,
a pair of drawers and breeches, and trowsers over
them ; two or three jackets, and a pair of new
shoes, and then filled my bosom and pockets as
full as I could well carry. Afterwards, I found it
was well for me that I did so ; for when the
clothes were brought on board, we found that all
the best of them had been culled out, and nothing
but a few rags and a dozen old blankets were sent
to us.

After we came on board, we were ordered upon
the quarter-deck, and from there down into the cable-tier, where we found very disagreeable lodgings, having nothing but the bare *cable* to lay upon, and that very uneven. Besides this, we were
almost suffocated with heat. Being, however,
very much fatigued, I slept about two hours, as
soundly as if I had been upon a bed of down. When
I awoke I crawled aft upon the cable, where was

the sentinel, and spent the remainder of the night in conversation with him.

In the morning the *boys* were called by the officers of the ship to come upon deck. Now, thinks I to myself, there is an advantage in being small. I'll embrace this opportunity, and try for my liberty upon deck, too. Accordingly, I went up, and no sooner were we on deck than we were thronged about by the seamen. They told us that a few hours after they took us, they spoke twelve or fourteen sail of transports, bound to New York, under convoy of a frigate, and she had thrown her guns overboard in a storm. I learned that the name of the Captain of the ship which had taken us, was Thomas Fitzherbert.

[The journal of the remainder of the passage to Plymouth, England, has been lost, and the next record commences some day or two after their arrival in this port.]

1777. January 15th. This morning our officers were brought on board again. We hear that the British troops have taken "Fort Washington," with the loss of *eight hundred men.*

16. A number of seamen's wives came on board to-day, and upon being told that they had American prisoners on board, " Have you ? " said one to the other; " What sort of people are they ? " " Are they white ? " " Can they talk ? "

Upon being pointed to where some of them stood, " Why ! " exclaimed they, " they look like our people, and they talk English."

17. Nothing remarkable.

18. To-day is the Queen's birth-day, and every ship in the harbor that is in commission, fired twenty-one guns, as a royal salute.

19. Sunday. To-day we were removed from the Reasonable to the Bellisle, a ship of sixty-four guns, after having been on board the Reasonable twenty-seven days. Here we lodged in the cable-tier, on boards laid over the cable, which is better than we had on board the Reasonable.

20. Nothing remarkable.

22. Last Sunday, " a prize " was brought in here, which proved to be the brig Triton, from Newburg, Captain Tileston, master. The captain was sent on shore and made his escape.

23. Nothing occurred worthy of notice.

24. To-day, two ships-of-war sailed from the sound. The Southampton, of thirty-six guns, and the Thetis, of thirty-two guns.

25. There has been a great market on board to-day.

26. Sunday. But very little respect paid to the day.

27. The daily allowance on board His Majesty's ships, is: Sunday, pork and peas; Monday, birgu,

butter and cheese ; Tuesday, beef and pudding ;
Wednesday, birgu and peas, butter and cheese ;
Thursday, pork and peas ; Friday, birgu and peas,
butter and cheese ; Saturday, beef and pudding ;
a pint of wine, or half a pint of rum, when at sea ;
and when in port, beer in abundance, and fresh
meat twice in a week.

28. To-day I received a pair of stockings, a
present from one of the seamen.

30. This morning, the captain, doctor and ser-
vant, of the privateer sloop Charming Sally,
from America, came on board this ship. They inform us that they were taken the 16th of January,
by the None-Such, man-of-war, sixty-four guns, and
have been well used ; having been on full allowance,
till they came on board this ship ; and the captain
that took them allowed them all their clothes and
bedding.

31. It is a time of general colds with us, and
about eighteen of our number are sick.

February 1. Windy, cold, blustering, unsteady
weather.

2. Nothing worthy of record.

4. We are told that orders have been received
from London, to repair all the prisons along
shore.

CHAPTER II.

FEBRUARY 5. It is a pay-day for bounty, on board this ship, (the Bellisle,) which occasions a great market on board.

6. We begin to grow very sickly, and twenty or thirty of us are suffering with the itch, and we are all dreadfully infested with vermin. I make a constant practice of examining my clothes every day, when we are permitted to go upon deck. I often find them swarming with these.

We are informed that the Admiral was heard to say, that no favor was to be shown to us, on account of our orders. We are also told by some, that we are to be removed, soon, on board the Ocean, which is the Admiral's ship; by others, that we shall be removed to prison.

This afternoon, about *one hundred* pressed men were brought on board this ship.

7. We were removed from the Bellisle, after having been on board nineteen days, and were carried up to Ammores, and put on board the "Tarbay," a ship of seventy-four guns, and confined in the bay, between decks, where there was not room for all of us to lay down; it is parted off, like a sheep-pen, and takes in two side-ports only.

8. Pleasant weather, but very cold for persons in our condition, as we are obliged to lay upon a wet deck, without either bedding or clothes, more than what we have on our backs — except a very few who have an old blanket apiece. As there is not room enough within our narrow quarters for every one to lay down at night, some are obliged to sit up all night.

9. There are now *sixteen* of our number on the doctor's list, and there are but very few of us but what are either complaining with bad colds or rheumatic pains; and if there are ten sick with as many different complaints, they give them all alike the same medicine.

10. Rough, cold, and some snow; all the way we have to keep ourselves warm, in the day time, is by play, and making ourselves merry.

11. We hear that General Lee is taken. I had to-day a handful of bread given to me by a woman, which I *joyfully* received.

12. We are informed that Parliament has passed an act that all Americans taken in arms against the King, shall be deemed rebels; and those taken in armed vessels, upon the high seas, as pirates.

13. Our company is in a very poor state of health. Last night I sat up with one at the point of death. We were removed to-day from the Tarbay, after being on board six days, and carried on board the Burford, a ship of *seventy-four* guns. Thanks be to God for this removal, for here we have more room, and there are but few men belonging to the ship besides the officers.

14. We are now on board the Burford, where we find better usage than we have received since we have been taken, and our sick have good care taken of them. We are also allowed to go upon deck, twenty at a time.

15. This morning sailed from Ammores three ships of the line, of seventy-four guns — the Albion, the Boyne and the Tarbay. To-day nine of our sick were carried on shore to the Royal Hospital. We were informed by one of the lieutenants of the ship, that, although their orders were to strip and plunder us, yet we should be allowed a bed and bedding, and such of us as had not clothes to change ourselves, should have them; which we may account as a favor.

16. Clear and pleasant, (Sunday,) and as we

are now between-decks, and have more room and
the light of the sun, and not confined to the
cable-tier, we have an opportunity for reading.

17. Very stormy. To-day we had delivered to
us, by the purser of the ship, bedding and clothes.
I received a shirt, and bedding, consisting of a
flock bed and pillows, a *rug*, and *blankets*. Some,
who were almost naked, had nearly a whole suit
given them. When they gave us the shirts, they
told us to take off our old ones and throw them
overboard, "lice and all."

18. Those of us who did not receive clothes
yesterday, have received them to-day, and those
who did not receive beds, are to receive them in
a few days. Our beds are a great comfort to our
sore bodies, after laying fifty-five nights without
any — all the time since we were taken — sometimes upon hard cables, sometimes upon boards
laid over the cables, and at other times on a wet
deck, with nothing to cover us but the clothes on
our backs. Now we have good bedding for our
comfort, thanks be to God! *and a good friend;*
for we are told that the captain of the ship, whose
name is Boyer, gave us these clothes and beds,
out of his own pocket.

19. This evening the remainder of our company received beds. We never know the true
state of our condition till it is illustrated by its

contraries; neither do we know how to value
what we have but by the want of it.

20. It is very sickly amongst us, and some one
is taken sick almost every day.

21. The Reasonable came out of dock and
dropped to her moorings. The Ocean is stripped
and going into dock. The Lizard, frigate, has
lately arrived from America, and to-day was towed
up from the Sound, having cut away her masts
yesterday in a gale of wind.

22. To-day a frigate sailed

CHAPTER III.

FEBRUARY 23. Sunday. We have an opportunity for reading.

24. Mr. Holland, the master-at-arms of the ship, has been on shore; he informs us of the death of one of our company — *Ebenezer Hunt.* He died on the 20th of this month, in the Royal Hospital; he was one of the nine that were sent on shore the 15th inst.

25. This morning Mr. Holland came into our apartment inquiring for a joiner. I offered myself, and went upon deck to work for him. He obtained the liberty of the carpenter's bench and tools, and I went to work, getting, also, permission for one of my acquaintances to come upon deck and work with me. We made him a table, for which

he gave us a bag to put our clothes in, half of a salt fish, a quart of potatoes, six biscuits, and butter to eat with our fish, besides a good hot supper.

26. I had an opportunity of reading a newspaper wherein was a confirmation, in several different places, of General Lee's being taken. I saw, also, an Act that was moved in Parliament and passed in the affirmative, 112 to 35; according to which we are guilty of high treason, and are sentenced to prison, there to lay, without bail, until the first of January, 1778, and then to have a trial.

> As we are prisoners in a cage,
>   It's our misfortune sure;
> 'T is folly to be in a rage,
>   Though hardships we endure.
>
> God grant that we may live to see
>   Once more our native place,
> For to enjoy our liberty,
>   Before we've run our race.

27. Last night the Boyne came up to her mooring, having sprung a leak and carried away her fore-topmast. She is the second, out of the three which sailed on the 15th inst., that has returned in distress. This ship's guns and carriages were brought alongside, and there were not men enough to hoist them in; so the captain sent his compliments to us, to see if we would assist in getting them on board, which we willingly did, because

he appears to be the best friend to us that we have met with since we have been taken.

28. We had a paper wherein is an account of the march and defeat of the King's troops towards Philadelphia, with the loss of fourteen or fifteen hundred men.

MARCH 1. Myself and one of my shipmates have again been upon deck to work. We made a chest for the master-at-arms, for which he gave us some biscuit. We mended, also, a table for the ship's cook, for which he gave us a supper and some spare bread and meat. It is in the paper that the ship which brought Dr. Franklin from Philadelphia to France, as she was returning, took a brig laden with fish, three days out of port, belonging to the same gentleman that bought the Dolton.

2. Prayers were read on board this ship to-day, and we were allowed to go on deck to hear them. A frigate arrived, after a six months' cruise, as we know by her firing a salute — which they are not allowed to do unless they have been six months absent. Myself and another have the liberty from the carpenter of the ship to work every day when we can get work to do.

26. It is four months since we sailed from Portsmouth, having been in that time twenty-eight days on board the Dolton, twenty-seven days on board

the Reasonable, nineteen on board the Bellisle, six on board the Tarbay, and forty-one on board the Burford, which is our present place of abode.

27. We are told that we are to go on shore to-morrow to prison. Our company, one after another, are daily dropping sick, and about forty of us have the itch; but our sick have as good care taken of them on board this ship as we could expect, and we are visited morning and evening by the doctor.

28. I have been poorly some days past, and having no appetite for my food I bought a quarter of a pound of sugar to sweeten some water gruel, which is the best that I can get here.

29. To-day two more were sent on shore to the Hospital, sick.

30. Sunday. But the time is badly spent for persons in our situation, who do not know how soon the gallows may be our doom.

31. I had sent to me, by the surgeon of the ship, about a pound of sugar and two ounces of tea, for some work which I did for him some time ago, and this morning I made some tea for my breakfast, which I drank with a good relish.

April 1. To-day I took an emetic of the doctor. There is another one of our company attacked with the *small-pox*, and to all human appearances, it will go through the company. I do not know that I ever can have it better than now, as I am well dieted, and therefore do not try to escape it.

2. To-day the Admiral and his lady, with several other ladies, came on board this ship to dine. This afternoon the man with small-pox was sent on shore, to the hospital.

3. Windy, cold weather. We hear that *three American* privateers went into Ireland, victualed and watered, and went out again, before it was known who they were.

4. This ship is bending her sails; it is reported that she is bound to sea soon. I suppose she is bound to Spithead, where a number from this place have gone.

5. Last evening the master-at-arms told us that we were to go on shore to-day at ten o'clock, but we are not there yet. To-day we had an opportunity of reading a newspaper, wherein is an account of the Americans taking nine hundred Hessian troops, on Christmas evening. As we are not allowed a paper, when we get one we are obliged to be very cautious how and when we read it.

6. Sunday. Again there has been prayers on board this ship, and a sermon preached. Another one of our company has broken out with the small-pox.

7. To-day the man with the small-pox was sent on shore.

8. There is another broken out with small-pox, and I expect every day to be attacked myself.

9. Two more of our company are quite unwell, and we expect it is small-pox. A lad who stole, and was obliged to run the gauntlet twice before, stole again, and to-day was punished in the same manner.

10. To-day three more were sent on shore with the small-pox, and three returned from the Hospital well, who were carried on shore the 15th of February. They tell us that they were used well. We hear that Captain Joseph Rowe has been taken in the ship "*Nancy*," from Newbury, and has been brought in here. He has now his liberty on shore, but his men are on board the Ocean, which is the Admiral's ship.

11. To-day the same lad who has stolen and run the gauntlet three times before, stole again; and we took another method with him. We tied him up, and our boatswain's mate gave him two dozen with the cat, on his bare back. At the least computation, in the three times which he run the gauntlet, exclusive of the punishment he received to-day, he must have had seven or eight hundred lashes, with hard nettles, on a bare back.

12. Pleasant weather. To-day *eight* more of

our company were carried on shore to the Royal Hospital, with the *itch*, and myself amongst the number. Alas! little did I think, six months ago, that I should ever set my foot on this island. It is four months and seventeen days since I left Portsmouth, all of which time I have been on the water. There are now twenty-four of our company in these hospitals, some with the small-pox, and the rest with the *itch*.

13. Sunday. I have been taking sulphur, to prepare for anointing this evening.

14. The first day I came here I was put upon diet; I had only half a pound of bread and a quart of milk, but now I am put on full allowance, which is a pound of beef, a pound of potatoes, and three pints of beer, per day.

15. We take a large spoonful of sulphur mixed with honey and cream tartar, morning and evening, and in the evening also use the ointment.

CHAPTER IV.

Royal Hospital Buildings — An Adventure — Taken down with Small-
pox — Three Prisoners escape — Re-taken — Severe Sickness —
Second Death — Joseph Hatch — Recovery — Kind attention of the
Nurses — Samuel Shriggings, the third of the company, died — Attempt to escape.

APRIL 16. Within these hospital wards there are *ten grand buildings*, three stories high. Each building contains six wards, each ward can accommodate twenty-five patients — so that there is room for fifteen hundred patients, besides attendants.

To-day our food, with our names entered in a book, was sent, which was headed, " Upon such a day a ward was opened for the *rebel prisoners ;* " I scratched out the word rebel and wrote American. When the book was returned, a messenger was sent with sixpence reward for any one who would tell who did it, but he returned no wiser than he came.

17. There are now fifteen of us in this ward,

and seven are upon what they call half-diet, (on account of their drawing coals and candles;) so that every other day we draw a half a pound of mutton, a pound of bread, a pound of potatoes, and a pound of greens.

18. To-day there are two more of our company brought on shore, with the itch.

19. I am very unwell; I have a bad pain in my head and back — the symptoms of small-pox — and the doctor ordered me something to take, immediately.

20. I have had six applications for the itch, but am not half cured; and to-day when the doctor came in to see me, he told me I had the small-pox, and ordered the nurse to remove me immediately, into the small-pox ward, which she did. After I got there, I was ordered to strip off all the dirty clothes that I had upon me. I washed myself in warm water, and put on a clean linen shirt, a woollen gown, waistcoat and drawers, and turned into bed with clean sheets.

21. I feel something better, and my pock comes out very fast; but it is the small sort, which is the worst.

Also, last evening three prisoners made their escape from the fifty-sixth ward, which is the same I left yesterday.

22. This morning got up, but my pock has come out exceedingly thick.

23. We are informed that the men who ran away are taken.

24. I am broken out so very thick, and the ointment for the itch inflamed my blood so much, that my flesh feels as if I was raked up in a bed of embers ; and I am so sick at my stomach that I vomit up every thing I eat, and am unable to write.

25. Kept my bed, and was in great pain.

26. My head was swollen very much, and I was so blind that I could scarcely see daylight.

27. My pock was almost to the full.

28. I feel easier as to pain.

29. My pock begins to turn.

30. I was very easy as to pain, but so very sore that I could scarcely lay in bed.

May 1. I got up, but was hardly able to walk.

2. I got up again, but my legs and feet swell very much.

3. To-day I feel something better.

4. I am some better, and got up again, but was unable to sit up long ; my pock begins to dry very well, and my swelling to go down.

5. This morning Joseph Hatch, one of our company, died with small-pox. He is the second of our company that has died in these hospitals.

6. I begin to grow bravely, and have a very good appetite for my victuals. I remain very sore, yet not so sore as I was two or three days ago; as my pock ran all together then, when I used to rise up in bed to receive any thing, and stuck to my linen and the sheets, so that it would tear off the scab from the whole length of my back, when I arose.

7. I am very sore yet, but am doing finely, considering that it is with some difficulty that I can get to the table to write; and I have a good appetite to eat. I asked the doctor for mutton, which he granted, so that I now have a pound of bread, half a pound of mutton, and a quart of beer.

8. There are two of our company now in this ward, very sick with the small-pox; but they have faithful care taken of them by the nurses, and the doctor is very kind. He allows them near half a pint of wine, or a small bottle of cordial, almost every day. The nurses, also, have been, and still are, *very kind to me.* When I first came into this ward, I brought a little tea and sugar with me, which I obtained on board the ships, and after it was all expended, the nurses gave me out of their own stores, tea twice a day, or as often as they make it for themselves.

[Mr. Herbert often in after life spoke in the highest terms of the kindness and attention of the nurses.]

9. Near half the scab has come off my body, and every morning when I get up, there is near a handful of scab left in the sheet, which comes off in the night.

10. I have several biles upon my legs, which cause a great deal of pain.

11. My legs are very sore, so that I am obliged to have them bound up from my ancles to my hips.

12. I am indifferently well, except my legs and thighs, where I have nearly a dozen biles, with which I am so lame I can scarcely walk.

13. To-day I took another portion of physic, which makes the sixth.

14. There are now twenty-six Americans here. Some are almost well of the small-pox, and have gone below into the recovering ward.

15. It is six months to-day since I left Newbury, and I fear it will be six more before I return.

16. To-day I took the seventh portion of physic.

17. This morning, died here, one Ebenezer Willis. He was a young man taken with Captain Brown, in the sloop Charming Sally. Also, this afternoon, of small-pox, Samuel Shriggings, he being the *third* of our company that has died in these hospitals, and the second in this ward, since I have been in it.

18. Last evening three of our company in the fifty-sixth ward, attempted to make their escape, but were discovered and taken before they got over the wall.

19. To-day I took my eighth portion of physic.

CHAPTER V.

Fourth Death — Captain Brown's Escape — His Men sent to Prison — Discharge from the Hospital — Yellow Fever — Fifth Death — Cruelty to the Dead — Examination — Commitment to Prison — Prison Allowance — Hunger — Prison Employments — Charity Box — Hard Fare — Guard Alarmed — Friendly Visitors — A Mean Trick.

MAY 20. There is a great frolic near by, called a bull-bating. We have a view of the people, but not of their sport.

We hear that the prisons are ready for the reception of the rebel prisoners, as we are called, and I daily expect our company to come on shore to them.

21. I gather strength, but as yet I am so weak as to be able to walk but very little. My chief employment is reading, but my eyes are weak, caused by rubbing them when I was almost blind.

22. There are two other Americans now in this ward, very sick with the small-pox; and one or two of our company, who are very sick.

23. I took my ninth portion of physic.

24. It is six weeks to-day since I came on shore, and five weeks to-morrow since I was brought into this building with small-pox. To-day I asked the doctor for some beef, which he granted; he also ordered me to go below into the recovering ward.

25. To-day I was upon full allowance, and drew a pound of beef, a pound of bread, a pound of potatoes, and three pints of beer.

26. This morning about seven o'clock, died James Jutson, an old man, prisoner from the Queen, taken with Captain Brown in the privateer sloop Charming Sally.

27. To-day we were forbidden the liberty of going up stairs to speak to our sick shipmates.

28. Yesterday, seven of Captain Brown's crew were sent to prison, from the ship, and Captain Brown made his escape from the "Fountain Tavern," in Plymouth Dock, where they were sent to be tried. Also, to-day took my tenth portion of physic.

29. To-day twelve of us were discharged from the hospital, but the boat did not come for us. We hear that the Bellisle has arrived in the Sound, has the yellow fever on board, and has been laid under quarantine, in the Sound, some time.

30. As we were discharged yesterday, and the boat did not come for us, to-day we were put upon

what they call cazzelteer, and only draw half a pound of bread and a quart of milk. A prisoner in the middle story, last night, being very sick with the small-pox, got out of his bed, threw up the window and jumped out. He fell head first, about twenty feet, upon the hard ground, bruising himself sadly.

31. It is now seven weeks since I came on shore, and six weeks to-day since I was brought here with small-pox.

June 1. It being pleasant weather, the nurse permitted me to walk in the garden.

2. We expected to have been removed, either to the ships or to prison, but were not.

3. To-day we were again discharged, but the boat did not come for us. Last night, one William Woodward, a prisoner, taken in the sloop Charming Sally, made his escape from this ward.

4. As we were discharged yesterday, and the boat did not come for us, we were again put upon cazzelteers and draw only a quart of milk, and a half pound of bread.

To-day is the King's birth-day, and there is great firing of cannon, and chiming of bells, in Dock and Plymouth.

This morning about three o'clock, another prisoner died of small-pox — the same person who jumped from the window, as before mentioned.

He was taken in the privateer sloop Charming Sally. After he was dead, his coffin was brought, which proved to be near six inches too short. But rather than have another made, they jammed him into that, in a most shocking manner.

5. This morning early, the boat came for us and twelve of us went on board and were carried along side the Blenheim, to which ship our company, and that of Captain Brown, had been removed since we went on shore. Four of the twelve that were in the boat belonged to the captain's crew. They were put on board the Blenheim, but the rest of us were carried on shore again, and guarded to the Fountain Tavern, to be tried by the judges; for that is the place where they sit. We were put into a small room, surrounded by a guard, and having eat nothing through the day, were very weak; so we got the soldiers to boil us a little meat, which we had obtained at the hospital. After this, we were all called up before the judges and examined. They asked each of us in what province we had been born, and whether or not we had a commission from Congress? At what time we entered on board the Dolton? Whether we were taken by the Reasonable? To each of their questions we answered. We were then sent below into the little room again; then we were called up the second time, one at a time, and asked

5

the same questions, to which we answered. They then read them over to us, and asked us if it was true, to which we replied it was. We told them we were out to fight the enemies of the thirteen United States.   After we were examined one by one, the third time, we were all called up together, as at the first, and our commitments were read to us and delivered to the constable.   My commitment read as follows :

"Charles Herbert, you are supposed to be guilty of the crime of high treason, and committed to prison for the same until the time of trial."

We were then delivered to the constable, and guarded to Old Mill Prison, Plymouth.

Alas ! I have entered the gates but the Lord only knows when I shall go out of them again.

June 6. Our allowance here in prison is a pound of bread, a quarter of a pound of beef, a pound of greens, a quart of beer and a little pot-liquor that the beef and greens are boiled in, without any thickening,— per day.

7. Pleasant weather, but we are kept in all day as a punishment for a misbeholden word spoken to the sentry on guard.

8. Sunday ; and there has been a great number of persons at the gate to see us, who gave in, for our relief, several shillings.

9. Rainy weather, so that we keep house all

day, except when we go out to draw our provisions.

10. There have about ten or twelve prisoners come from the ships to prison to-day. Having so lately had the small-pox, and being so long physiced afterwards, I require more victuals now, than I ever did before; and our allowance is so very small, and having only sevenpence left of what little money I had when I came to prison, I had a continual gnawing at my stomach; and I find that unless I take some method to obtain something more than my bare allowance, I must certainly suffer, if not die, and that soon. As necessity is the mother of invention, I am resolved to try to get something, and to-day when a carpenter came to put in a window at the end of the prison, I entreated him to bring me some deal, and I would make him a box, which he did.

11. To-day we have made a charity-box, and put it up at the gate. There is written upon it, "Health, Plenty, and Competence to the donors." I have finished the box for the carpenter, and he likes it so well that he wants more made, and he brought me some more wood for that purpose, — some for him, and some for myself.

12. I have been busy all day making boxes, and some of the prisoners are making punch ladles, spoons, chairs, and the like; for which they, now and then, get a shilling.

13. We have chosen a purser amongst ourselves to take charge of the avails of the charity-box. Some days we get four or five shillings, and upon others, not more than four or five pence.

14. To-day we drew only half a pound of greens. They tell us it is by the order of the board ; our meat is very short, and our broth only the pot-liquor with the fat skimmed off.

15. Last night the guard was alarmed. They supposed that they heard noises as if we were breaking out of prison; this is the second time this guard has been alarmed when we were all silent.

16. Wet weather, so that we keep house.

17. I have been employed for several days past, making boxes, and carving them. To-day I sold two, one for a shilling, the other for ninepence.

18. To-day there have been several gentlemen and ladies to see us, and they gave us several small books ; I sold, also, another box for a shilling.

19. There is one of the prisoners who has been unwell for several days, and is now broke out with the small-pox.

20. There are about ten prisoners brought to prison nearly every day; but there are only a few more to come.

21. I have now got into such a way of making boxes and selling them, that I can afford to buy myself a breakfast every morning; commonly

bread and milk, which is brought to prison every morning for sale.

22. Sunday; there have been great numbers of people to see us, and the prison guard, confederating with the turnkey, have got a box put up at the gate, and they will let no one look in to see us, without paying in a certain amount. To-day we are told that they got fifteen shillings in their box, which they divided among themselves; but the people who put it in thought it was for the prisoners. We, therefore, took in our box, and are resolved to put it out no more.

CHAPTER VI.

JUNE 23. To-day we divided the money which
we had got in our charity-box, and it was only five
farthings per man.

24. To-day there were two more prisoners
brought in ; they were taken in France. Having
been invited on board an English vessel, and not
knowing who they were, went on board, and were
immediately seized and confined. The vessel
then weighed anchor and came out of the harbor.
The prisoners proved to be the captain and lieutenant of a Virginia pilot boat. The captain is
now confined in the yard, in a prison by himself,

and is not allowed to speak to us, but the lieutenant is in prison with us.

25. Rainy weather.

26. Continued wet, so that we keep house.

27. To-day another broke out with small-pox.

28. To-day Captain Ross, one of our prizemasters, had a present of some bread and cheese.

29. Sunday. To-day there have been great numbers to see us, but they were disappointed; for they kept the outer gate shut, and would not let the people look at us.

30. We are so confined here that we are out of the way of all news; we are not allowed a newspaper, and at present no one is allowed to come to the gate to speak to us. The week past, I have received three shillings and two pence, for boxes.

July 1. Nothing remarkable.

2, 3. Very rainy, so that we are obliged to keep house.

4. Fair weather. This is the only fair day we have had for nearly a week; and to-day a fleet of transports with troops, bound to America, put in here for a harbor.

5. To-day several American gentlemen came to see us. They came to England before the war began; they gave considerable money to some with whom they were acquainted; to one they gave *two* guineas, to another *one*, to another half

a guinea, and to three more five shillings apiece. The week past I have received one shilling and two pence for boxes.

6. Sunday. A great number of persons came to see us, but the gate was kept shut, so they could not speak to us, or give us any thing; but some that were in prison took a small bag and tied a string to it and let it down at a window at the back side of the prison. About a sixpence was put into it, but the guard came in and forbid it.

7. They have placed lanterns all round the prison yard, for fear that some of us should make our escape in the night.

8. Last night the guard became alarmed by our people laughing and singing, and they came in and took one of the prisoners to the *Black-hole*, a place of punishment so called, where he is to lay *forty days*, on half allowance, and nothing to sleep on but the ground. We were all threatened to be put on half allowance. This afternoon there sailed from the Sound a fleet of transports of about thirty sail, and three convoys, bound to America. According to the best accounts, there are about four thousand troops on board.

9, 10, 11. Warm and pleasant weather. Nothing remarkable.

12. Last night, four of the prisoners that were

in the hospital, one that was in the Black-hole, and one from a prison where there are a number using applications for the itch, made their escape through a drain that leads to the river edge. For this week past I have received three shillings and six-pence for boxes and ladles.

13. Sunday. Those who remain in the itch apartment are all put on half allowance, to make them tell which way the man got out who made his escape from that building; and a sentinel is set before the prison to keep us from giving them any thing, or speaking to them.

14. The Yarmouth, a ship of seventy-four guns, dropped down into the Sound, in order for sailing.

15. The prisoners in the itch apartment told the agent which way the man got out of prison, and were put upon their usual allowance.

16. We hear of the death of Thomas Rines, one of our company, whom I left sick at the Royal Hospital; he died of the small-pox, and is the fourth of our company who has died since we were taken.

17. Several in prison have broken out with the small-pox, all of whom inoculated themselves from the first that were attacked with it.

18. There has been a great deal of talk of a French war ever since we have been taken, and it appears now to be very near, for the English ves-

sels are often receiving insults at sea from the
French.   Three years ago they would have re-
sented this, but now they appear to be afraid.

19. The remainder of the prisoners who have
not had the small pox have had an offer from the
doctor to be inoculated.

20. Last night we made a breech in the prison
wall, and began to dig out, which we expect will
take near a fortnight to accomplish, as we have
near eighteen feet to dig under ground to get into
a field on the other side of the wall.

21. For the week past I have received, for boxes and ladles, two shillings and sixpence.

22. The hole that is now in hand is to be only
just large enough for a man to crowd himself out.
The men that dig it have made great progress
since they have been at work ; we put all the dirt
into our chests, as we have several of them in
prison, and when they leave work they stop up the
hole with the same stones that came out, and
daub it over with lime, so that it appears like the
other wall.

23. Last evening transports arrived here from
America, with six hundred wounded marines on
board.

24. We had a present sent us of several pounds
of leaf tobacco.

25. To-day three of the number who broke out

A NEWSPAPER FROM HOME. p. 58.

of the sick ward, on the 12th of this month, were brought back again, and put in the Black-hole, there to lay forty days, on half allowance.

26. We hear that Captain Manley, of the Hancock frigate, has taken the Fox frigate, of twenty-eight guns.

27. For the week past I have received eighteen-pence for boxes.

29. The remainder of the prisoners who have not had the small-pox, removed into a seperate building, in order for inoculation.

30. Although we are not allowed newspapers, yet we have them almost weekly, and we now have one that gives an account of the before mentioned frigate being taken; also of Captain Giddson, in the " Civil Usage," being seen off the Lizzard.

August 1. To-day six more of our people came on shore from the ship; the occasion of their not being brought to prison sooner was, that they were detained with small-pox in the Royal Hospital. One of these is yet very unwell, and has been put in the prison hospital.

2. We learn, by those who came in yesterday, that Captain Adams, who was taken in a merchantman, was set at liberty last Sunday. The week past I have received two shillings for boxes.

3. Sunday. The number of prisoners now in these wards, is one hundred and seventy-three.

4. Some of our people who first broke out with small-pox in prison, are so far recovered as to be able to come up from the hospital.

5. Pleasant to-day, but stormy last night; during the storm, some of our people made their escape through the hole which they began to dig on the nineteenth of last month. This hole is dug eighteen feet under ground, and comes up in a field the other side of the wall. Thirty-two in number went out, three of whom have been brought back. We are told that they have five pounds bounty for taking up any rebel prisoner that attempts an escape; and when taken, the prisoners are to be put on half allowance, and placed in the Black-hole for forty days.

6. To-day one more was brought back that went out night before last.

7. Four more were brought in to-day, so that there are eight out of the thirty-two taken already. The four who were brought back to-day are put in with us, as the Black-hole is full, but they will be put on half allowance, the same as if in the Black-hole.

8. The guards are now so very suspicious of us, that they number us two or three times a day,

and visit us as often by night; and once or twice they will overhaul all our chests to see that there is no dirt in them, or any tools secreted that we can dig out with. To-day an old man was put into the Black-hole for only complaining that our meat was not good.

9. To-day there was one more brought back that passed under the wall. For the week past I have received three shillings for boxes.

10. We hear that an American privateer is taken.

11. To-day nine more prisoners came on shore to the prison from the Blenheim Eight of the number were taken in one of Captain Weeks' prizes, bound to France; the other was one of our company, who has been sick at the Royal Hospital. They inform us that Captain John Lee is taken in the brig Fancy, twelve guns, fitted out at Newbury, belonging to the Traceys, and forty-two of his hands came on board the Blenheim before they left her. To-day two more were brought back who went out at the hole.

12. To-day eight more prisoners came to the prison from the Blenheim; three of the number were taken in the Fancy with Captain Lee. They inform us that they were chased on shore at Mount Bay, near Land's-end, by the Fieutryant, a ship of eighty-four guns. They are only about

eight weeks from America, and had taken four prizes.

13. Ten more of Captain Lee's men came to prison.

14. Ten more were brought to-day.

15. To-day Captain Lee and his first and second lieutenants came to prison. From Captain Lee I hear of the health of my friends.

16. A number more of Captain Lee's men came to prison to-day.

17. Sunday. For the week past I have received six shillings and three pence for boxes and ladles.

18. Warm and pleasant, so that we carried our hammocks out into the yard to air. The remainder of Captain Lee's men were brought to prison. Those who came to-day were the last who were taken after they got on shore. They inform us that they are all here now except their doctor, who, in all probability, has made his escape.

19. To-day three more were brought to prison who belonged to the Literal Mark, fitted out of Philadelphia.

20. Warm and pleasant weather, so that we can comfortably go barefoot; but many of us would be obliged to do so if it were in the middle of winter, for want of stockings and shoes.

21. To-day fourteen of Captain Lee's men,

who have not had the small-pox, were inoculated. The prisoners who are on half allowance have had a meal of victuals sent them by some friend.

22. We hear that Ticonderoga is taken by the King's troops, and also Philadelphia; that the Hancock, Captain Manley, is taken, and the Fox retaken; but we cannot tell what to believe by what we hear; for since we have been taken we have heard, nearly twenty times, that Philadelphia was taken, and as many times that Washington was killed; that Congress was divided, that continental money was disgraced, that the Americans had laid down their arms, and that they were starving to death for want of provisions, and naked for want of clothing; all these things have been published in the newspapers, times without number, since we have been taken.

23. For the week past I have received three shillings for boxes.

24: Sunday. This is the greatest market day for our wooden ware, as most people come on this day to see us.

25. Yesterday Daniel Cottle died in the prison hospital of the small-pox; he is the sixth of our company that has died since we have been in England.

26. It is reported that general Prescott is taken by the Americans.

CHAPTER VII.

AUGUST 27. Last night, as our people who are
on half allowance in a separate prison, were trying to dig out, the guard went in and caught them.
Two of these are now confined in the Black-hole.
To-day a prize was brought in here ; she appears
to be a small brig.

30. For the week past, I have received four
shillings for boxes.

31. Sunday. To-day we had a newspaper, wherein was a confirmation of Ticonderoga and Philadelphia being taken ; also, of the Hancock frigate
and Fox being retaken ; this news is very disagreeable to us, for we are sorry to hear of the en-

emy being in any way victorious; for should they conquer the country, or even get the upper hands of it, we are positive that the gallows or the East Indies will be our destiny. But as to conquering the country, it never disturbed, for me, an hour's rest, though it appears that they are in a fairer way for doing it now, than ever before. We have trouble enough here, without hearing bad news; for it is enough to break the heart of a stone to see so many strong, hearty men, almost starved to death through want of provisions. A great part of those in prison, eat at one meal what they draw for twenty long hours, and then go without until the next day. Many are strongly tempted to pick up the grass in the yard, and eat it, and some pick up old bones in the yard, that have been laying in the dirt a week or ten days, and pound them to pieces and suck them. Some will pick up snails out of the holes in the wall, and from among the grass and weeds in the yard, boil them and eat them, and drink the broth. Often the cooks, after they have picked over our cabbage, will cut off some of the but-ends of the stalks and throw them over the gate into the yard, and I have often seen, after a rain, when the mud would be over shoes, as these stumps were thrown over the gate, the men running from all parts of the yard, regardless of the mud, to catch at them, and nearly trample

6

one another under feet to get a piece. These same
cabbage stumps, hogs in America would scarcely
eat if they had them; and as to our broth, I know
very well hogs in America would scarcely put their
noses into it.   Our meat is very poor in general ;
we scarcely see a good piece once in a month.
Many are driven to such necessity by want of provisions, that they have sold most of the clothes off
their backs for the sake of getting a little money to
buy them some bread. I find it very hard, myself,
but it is not so hard with me and a few others, who
have got into a way of making boxes and punch
ladles, for which we get a trifle, as it is with the
prisoners, in general, who are obliged to live upon
their allowance ; but I expect that boxes and punch
ladles will soon become an old thing, for many
who buy them now, buy them more out of charity
than any thing else.

September 1. Nothing remarkable, but repeated confirmation of the before-mentioned sad
news.

2. We are informed by a friend, that he is fearful that we shall be distributed on board of His
Majesty's ships.

3. There is one of our company who lays very
ill with small-pox, but all Captain Lee's men, who
were inoculated, are better.

4. Last night Gideon Warren, one of our com-

pany, died of small-pox, in the prison hospital. He is the sixth of our company who has died since we were taken — five of the number died of small-pox.

5. To-day the carpenters have been at work, altering the hanging of our hammocks, to make them hang on the middle rail, for fear that we should make a breach in the wall and conceal the same by our hammocks hanging against it until we make our escape.

6. For the week past, I have received one shilling and ninepence, for boxes.

7. Sunday. We were threatened to be put on half allowance, on account of the orders being torn, which are put up in the prison.

8. Several who have recovered from small-pox, came up from the hospital.

9. To-day two large ships sailed from the Sound.

10. This morning, early, while some of our people were digging out, the guard came upon them, and we were all immediately turned out and searched, and all our knives taken from us, that they could find; some other tools, and some paper which they found in prison, as we are not allowed paper, pens or ink ; but I passed the search with two knives and my journal about me. Captain Bird, captain of a packet bound to America,

came to see us, and offered to carry letters for us.

11. Eleven of Captain Lee's men came up from the hospital, recovered from the small-pox, after being inoculated.

12. To-day a commissioner came here from London. He told us, with other business, he came to see us righted about our provisions; he said that he lodged twenty-five miles distant last night, on purpose to be here at the time of our drawing our provisions. He also gave us liberty, whenever we wished to make our grievances known, to write to the Board, without inspection by the agent.

13. To-day we wrote our petition to the Board, for redress of grievances, and it was read before the prisoners. Also, we had a paper, wherein was a melancholy account of the barbarous treatment of American prisoners, taken at Ticonderoga, and an account of the Indians in Burgoyne's army proving treacherous.

14. Sunday. The week past I have received three shillings for boxes.

15. For nearly a month past, the carpenter, of whom I have had my wood, has not been here, so that I have been working a chest up into boxes, on shares. When finished and sold, it brought nearly thirty-two shillings; but I have had a partner to work with me, and one third of the avails

we paid for the chest, so that only one third belonged to myself.

16. Mr. Bell, the commissioner, has been here again, and measured our cans, in which we draw our beer, and he says he shall come again and try the weights and measures by which we draw our provisions. To-day about twenty old countrymen petitioned the Board for permission to go on board His Majesty's ships.

17. To-day the bells have been chiming in Plymouth and Dock, on the election of a new Lord Mayor.

18. Yesterday some friends, from without, sent victuals to those men who are on short allowance, but the agent would not let them come in.

19. The commissioner has again been here; he came precisely at the time of drawing our meat. We complained to him about the market, and he told us that no one should be allowed to retail any thing out to us, but that there should be an open market at the gate, three hours in a day. Also, those knives that were taken away a few days ago, were handed in again.

20. For the week past, I have received one shilling and eightpence for boxes.

21. Sunday. Last evening about nine o'clock, it being very dark, a number attempted to get over the wall by the help of a line, but as the sixth man

was getting over, they were discovered, and three of the number immediately taken.

22. To-day is the King's coronation day, and each ship in commission, in the harbor, fired a salute.

23. To-day the masons have been at work, building the wall higher where the men got over.

24. Pleasant weather.

25. We are informed that the Lexington, privateer, Captain Henry Johnston, of sixteen guns, is taken by a cutter of ten guns.

26. Last evening one of our company made an attempt to get over the wall, but no sooner was he over than he was discovered and taken. The commissioner again visited us, and spoke in particular to each of our requests. He informed us that a newspaper could not be allowed us, and that persons on half allowance must not be helped by any donations; he told us that he had written to the Board for an addition of a quarter of a pound of beef to a man; and as cold weather was coming on, for shoes and stockings for such as are destitute. Since this gentleman has been in town, our provisions have been much better than they were before. This afternoon, Captain Johnston, of the Lexington privateer, and six of his officers, were brought to prison in a coach.

27. Ten more of Captain Johnston's men came

to prison to-day. They inform us that they were taken by a ten gun cutter after almost four hours' engagement, and having expended all their shot; they were so disabled by having their shrouds, stays, and braces shot away, and so nearly wrecked, that they were obliged to strike to their inferiors. They had six men killed and a number wounded; their first lieutenant had an arm shot off, and after they were taken they were not stripped as our company had been, but were allowed all their clothes; and Captain Johnston was allowed even to wear his hanger, which he brought to prison with him, and delivered to the agent. He had considerable money with him, which the agent took, and he is to have it in small quantities as he wants it, for immediate use.

28. Sunday. Two large men-of-war came up from the Sound to Ammoors; also, a frigate arrived in the Sound, dismasted.

29. Michaelmas day.

30. Within a few days, three East Indiamen arrived here, and we are told that a great part of their men are pressed on board of the men-of-war. This afternoon a number more of Captain Johnston's men were brought to prison.

October 1. A number more of Captain Johnston's men came to prison; they inform us that

the Frenchmen which they had on board, are not
likely to come to prison.   There were about twenty of them.

3. Captain Lee, being unwell, was sent to the
hospital.

4. To-day the remainder of Captain Johnston's
men came to prison, except the Frenchmen.

5. Sunday.   Pleasant weather.

6. To-day one of our company was brought
back, who made his escape over the wall on the
20th of last month.   This is the fourth time that
this man has tried to escape without success.

7. The father and mother of one of Captain
Lee's men came to see him; they had not seen
each other before, for nearly fifteen years.

8. One of the officers of the Fieutryant came to
prison to see Captain Lee.   He informed us that
they have been cruising two hundred and fifty
leagues to the westward, and have taken one of
the schooner Hawk's prizes.

9. When the commissioner was here, we requested of him the privilege of two men per day,
to go into the cook-room and cut up our meat,
and see it put into the copper, which he granted.

10. Warm and pleasant.

11. To-day the captains of the Burford and
Fieutryant came to see us.

12. Sunday. Of late, there have not been so many people to see us as formerly.

13 To-day our agent has been in a very good humor, and he informed us that there is great expectation of a French war, and within a few days there have been four ships of the first class put in commission, and orders have come from London to man them as quickly as possible. He also tells us that he has had a letter from the commissoner, which says that Mr. Knapp, and another Newbury man, who made their escape from this place on the 5th of August last, are taken up.

14. To-day a mess of us bought a bag of potatoes, containing seventeen gallons, for three shillings, which is much cheaper than to buy them at the gate for fourpence a gallon.

15. It is eleven months to-day since we sailed from Newburyport.

16. To-day a Marblehead man came to see us, who has been on board the men-of-war ever since the disturbance. He informs us that there are a few Marblehead men on board the Blenheim.

17. This afternoon there were seven more prisoners brought on shore to prison; some of whom belong to the schooner Hawk's prize, that was taken by the Fieutryant, and the rest belong to the Oliver Cromwell privateer, that was taken by the Beaver sloop-of-war.

7

18. We learn by those who came to prison last,
that Dr. Franklin has written to the English ambassador, concerning an exchange of prisoners.

19. Sunday.   This morning we found out that
one of our company, confederate with a black
man, had stolen, last night, an allowance of bread
and cheese from those who came last to prison, —
for which they made him run the gantlet up
one side of the prison and down the other, one
hundred and thirty feet, through a double file of
men armed each with a nettle.

CHAPTER VIII.

October 20. There has been a prospect of a
French war ever since we have been taken, but
now I believe it is inevitable.

21. To-day we have drawn new hammocks,
which are nearly a foot shorter than those we had
before, on account of the hanging of them being
altered.

22. To-day the remainder of the prisoners came
on shore to the prison, and among them is a
young man belonging to one of the schooner
Hawk's prizes. This young man formerly lived

with Thomas Tennant, of Newbury. From him I obtained intelligence of the health of my father and brother, and many other friends. It is a great satisfaction to me to hear from home, though it is very uncertain whether or not I ever see it.

23. Wet weather.

24. Warm and pleasant.

25. King Charles' restoration day. The garrison, fort, and each ship in the harbor, in commission, fired a salute. We are told that twelve sail of the line have been put in commission within a few days. We learn that there are suspicions that a French fleet has gone to the West Indies. To-day a large ship came in here in distress, having carried away her main-mast and mizen-topmast.

26. It is eleven months to-day since we left Portsmouth.

27. Last night two prisoners, Cutter and Morris, made their escape from the prison hospital; also to-day another prisoner ran the gantlet for stealing a penny loaf from one of the prisoners.

28. We are informed that two sentries, who were knowing to those two prisoners making their escape, are confined upon suspicion, and one of them has turned King's evidence, and informed of the other.

29. Cold and windy weather.

30. A bad storm, so that we keep house all day, except when we get out to draw our provisions.

31. Pleasant and warm, for the season.

November 1. We are informed that a few days ago, in a storm, a ship appeared, at a small distance from land, and gave a signal of distress, and in about ten hours was not to be seen; it is supposed she foundered.

2. We are informed that there is as hot a press now going on as ever was known in England; and that fifteen hundred seamen are wanted immediately, to fit out a fleet.

3. We have a paper, dated the 21st of last month, wherein is an account of General Burgoyne's losing two thousand men, besides a number taken prisoners.

5. To-day is Gunpowder Treason, and they make but little account of it compared with what I expected. To-day a boy ran the gantlet, for stealing.

6. To-day some prisoners, in a separate prison, who have been trying for some time to make their escape by digging out, were discovered by the guard.

7. We have a paper wherein are several fine pieces in behalf of America, which I hope will prove of advantage, as the Parliament is to set about the 15th or 20th of this month; I am per-

suaded that the American affairs will be called up
as the first question, and the subject of the most
importance.

8. Two ships-of-war dropped down into the
Sound, in order for sailing.

9. Sunday.   Somewhat cold, and there are a
great many in prison who have neither shoes nor
stockings for their feet, and scarcely a jacket or
shirt for their back: these must inevitably suffer, if not perish, this winter, with cold, if not
supplied with clothing.   As to myself, I have
enough to keep me comfortable as to clothes,
which is more than two-thirds in prison have; for
many have been obliged to sell their clothes to buy
provisions.

10. To-day six persons, in a separate prison, as
they were at work in a drain under ground, digging out, were discovered by the guard, and
caught in the drain, and carried to the Black-hole.

11. Two of the turnkeys, who used to tend the
doors and gates, have been discharged; I suppose on suspicion of their being too good friends
to us.

12. To-day an American captain, belonging to
Manchester, who was taken in a merchantman,
came to see us.   He is set at liberty, and is bound
home.   Several in prison sent letters by him, but

we could not write a true account, because our letters were examined.

13. Wet weather. Our yard, which was a pleasant spot when we came into it, is now nearly a mud pond in wet weather, and in dry a dust heap.

14. This morning, as some in prison were at work, trying to dig out, the guard came in and found the hole; and when they came to turn us out, there were one or two who did not move so soon as they wanted them to do, and they struck and abused them; afterwards, when one of the prisoners went to one of the prison windows to look for something, the sentry in the prison yard saw him and struck him over the back, and broke his bayonet.

15. It is twelve months to-day since we sailed from Newburyport. I hope the Lord in whom we ought to trust, will, in his own good time, deliver us out of the hands of our enemies, and return us to a free country, — which would be a day of good fortune, a day of agreeable surprise and great joy. Then would I say —

> Thrice happy youth, though destitute and poor,
>   These are my restoration days ;
> The Lord, who brought me out, I'm sure
>   Can teach me how his name to praise.

16. Sunday. Pleasant for the season of the year.

17. This day I am twenty years of age. I have often read in authors of some great transaction to be laid open to the world in the year 1777, and I have been looking for it, in hope of seeing the event; but, alas! little did I think that at the age of twenty years I should have spent almost a twelvemonth of my time a prisoner.

18. It has been reported for several days past, that Philadelphia is taken. I believe I may assert with truth, that since we have been taken, we have heard fifty times that Philadelphia was taken, and often I have seen it in the papers, and many people believe it. It is in this manner that the poor and common people in England are blinded, by false reports; and some of the gentlemen of Plymouth hired the sexton to ring the bells, for rejoicing.

19. Captain Lee received a letter from Bilboa, and had an offer of being supplied with money. This letter informs us that Mr. Stevanson, Captain Lee's lieutenant, who made his escape from prison on the 21st of September, has arrived safe in Bilboa.

20. This morning William Moody, a Newbury man, taken with Captain Tileston about nine months ago, came to see us. He has got inva-

lided, and intends to make the best of his way home.

21. We are told that six more large ships have been put in commission.

22. Our bread to-day is intolerably bad; it appears to us as though it was made of the grain of malt, or chopped straw: there are straws in it an inch long, and it is so hully and tough, that it is scarcely fit for a beast to eat. We complained of it, and were told if we would put up with it to-day we should have no more such.

23. Sunday. There are so many men in the prison, and so few books, that, in general, we are but poorly employed

24. We hear that there has a packet arrived from America, but we shall not learn what news she brings, until their contents have been to London and refined.

25. We hear that Captain Thompson, of the Bailey frigate, is now in France.

26. It is twelve months to-day since we sailed from Portsmouth. It is enough to vex the spirit of any man, to think that such a number of men should be thrown away, and brought into trouble through the misconduct of one man. If there had been good conduct on board of our vessel, we should have made up our cruise in twenty-four hours from the time we were taken; for, that

same night, in a few hours after we were taken, the Reasonable spoke twelve or fifteen sail of transports bound to America, and their convoy had thrown their guns overboard in a storm.

27. We are informed that the King's Speech is in the papers, and that he is resolved to carry on the war with America, at all hazards.

28. For the two months past I have received ten shillings for boxes. Ever since about ten days after I came to prison, I have bought myself a breakfast of bread and milk, every morning it was to be had ; and of late I have had potatoes to eat with my meat almost every day, which, I am sorry to say, is more than two thirds in prison can get.

29. To-day I had an opportnnity of reading the King's Speech to the House of Lords, on the 20th of this month, in which he acknowledges that he is much grieved at the great expense the nation is at in this war ; but he hopes that the Parliament will assist him still in carrying it on with vigor.

30. Sunday. Last evening, it being very dark and stormy, we were in general resolved to put in execution a plan proposed — to dig out at the back side of the prison, seize the sentry, confine him, and carry him out of call, but not to hurt him. Upon breaking ground, they unexpectedly saw a lamp placed near the hole, which gave light all round, so that they thought it impracticable to

put their design into execution. I think if it had been otherwise, nearly two thirds in prison would have gone out. I got myself dressed and ready, and was in hopes of getting out, but to my sorrow, I find myself still in Mill Prison.

December 1. I had an opportunity of hearing the paper read, which gives an account of General Lee being exchanged; but for my own part, I do not expect we shall be exchanged before the conclusion of the war, unless France and Spain declare war, which to appearance, cannot be avoided.

2. We are informed that two packets have lately arrived, and confirm the reports that Philadelphia is taken. Also, they have reported that the Amercans have blown up an English seventy-four, which was attempting to go up to Philadelphia.

3. This morning the guard discovered another hole which we begun to dig yesterday. I think we have been very diligent and careful to improve every opportunity to make our escape, but the guard is so very strict with us, that I think it almost impossible to succeed, and we have reason to think that there are some traitors amongst us, who give information of every thing of the kind which we undertake.

4. We, in our mess, bought another bag of patatoes, for three shillings.

5. This day twelvemonth I was at sea in a
storm ; the same day, by what I can learn, was a
day of thanksgiving in America.

6. Last evening, a man in prison received a letter from a friend in London, which desired him
to make himself easy, for we should be delivered
before we were aware of it ; but we have been told
such stories ever since we have been in England ;
so we place very little confidence in it.

7. Sunday. It is a great grievance to be shut
up in prison, and debarred from hearing the gos-
pel preached on the Lord's day, though I did not
make much improvement of it when I had the opportunity.

8. To-day we were all mustered, and after this
was over, the agent informed us that he had received a letter from the Board, to put all in this
prison on half allowance, for breaking orders and
attempting to make our escape, until the trans-
gressor should be found out. But as we all, with
one voice joined in one cause, we thought it inhuman to pitch upon any one man ; therefore, by way
of contribution, we raised money enough to hire
one man to own the same and suffer for all, so that
we are obliged to support him while on half allowance and make him amends for his sufferings

9. To-day the man delivered himself up, to go
to the Black-hole, and the agent allows him every

indulgence consistent with his orders, which is a very uncommon thing for him.

10. Warm and pleasant, for the season of the year.

11. There have been various reports for several days past, but I thought them not worthy of observation, because they did not come from so good authority as I could wish they might; but to-day he have a very authentic account from Captain Henry Johnston's brother, who is lately from London, that General Burgoyne and his army are totally routed, many killed, and taken to a man; and as I do not doubt the truth of it, it gives me more satisfaction than any news I have heard since I have been a prisoner. Also, we have good reason to believe that Howe is in possession of Philadelphia; but Washington, of choice, without any molestation, let him march in, for we hear that the Americans have possession of all the forts on the river.

12. I purchased a book called the " American Crisis," on purpose to lend it to a friend without. We are told that the generality of the people in England are very much disaffected at the proceedings of the ministry.

13. To-day we all carried our clothing out into the yard, and were examined to know who wanted clothes, and who did not. But for my part, I am not in need of any thing, for with what little

money I have got in time past, by making boxes, I
have clothed myself tolerably well. We were told,
by a gentleman who came to see us, that our countrymen at home have something to be proud of,
though we are a little humbled by our imprisonment.

14. To-day Captain Lee received a letter from
Captain Trott, who was taken in one of the Civil
Usage's prizes.   He informs us of their taking ten
valuable prizes, and six of the number were arrived safely at the place of destination.

15. Cold weather to what it has been for some
days past.

16, 17. We have a paper wherein is a confirmation and the particulars of General Burgoyne's
being taken, with six thousand men, seven thousand stand of arms, seven thousand suits of clothes,
seventy thousand guineas, sixty batteaux, with a
thousand barrels of provisions, and a great many
pieces of artillery, which in England they ac-
knowledge to be the best ever sent out of the country, against any nation.   We have, also, a melancholy account of the cruelty of the Indians in the
back settlements, set on by the inhuman Burgoyne, and an account of General Lincoln's taking
two forts, up North River, and putting the people
to the sword. We hear, besides, of General Washington's giving Howe battle, and after the battle

was over, there were six hundred wagon loads of dead and wounded seen to go into Philadelphia. After hearing this news, joy is plainly seen in the countenance of every American here.

18. We hear that Lord North has made a motion for peace, in the House, but they thought as he was one of the chief instigators of war, that he had no right to have any hand in making peace.

19. We hear that General Putnam had intercepted several letters sent by Howe to Burgoyne, which showed their determination, and proved of happy consequences to the Americans. According to the last accounts, the American loss in the late engagements is very inconsiderable.

20. To-day six men came up from the Black-hole, who were sent there on the tenth of last month — their forty days having expired.

21. Nothing remarkable, except repeated confirmations of what we have heard before.

22. We are informed that Parliament has adjourned till the twentieth of next month ; I suppose, to hear further intelligence from Lord Howe, and to know whether he has made any progress in the country.

CHAPTER IX.

DECEMBER 23. To-day we have new printed orders put up in prison, which are from the commissioners, to be strictly observed by us.

24. It is twelve months since I was taken, and
as to-morrow is Christmas, and we have a little
money, we are resolved to have something more
than we had last Christmas; accordingly we sent
out for five pounds of flour, one pound of suet, one
pound of plums, half a pound of sugar, half an
ounce of spice, and two quarts of milk, to mix the
same for a pudding.

25. Christmas. To-day had our intended pudding, and as there was so much of it that we could not conveniently boil it all in one bag, we made two of it, and the largest was as much as seven of of us wanted to eat at one meal, with our other provisions; these seven were of our own mess, and three of our neighbors, whom we invited. To-day our baker, who supplies us with bread, instead of brown bread, sent us white, and our butcher, instead of beef, gave us mutton, and instead of cabbage we had turnips; and the butcher's wife gave us oatmeal to thicken our broth, and salt to salt it; so that on the whole, we had not so hungry a Christmas as the last. I must confess I have a very agreeable expectation, if my life is spared and the Lord pleases to permit me, to sit down at my father's table next Christmas.

26. To-day considerable bread was given in the yard, by gentlemen who visited us, besides a penny loaf to each mess, sent in by our friends outside.

27. For some days I have been unwell, and this morning I took a portion of salts.

28. Sunday. Warm weather, as it is natural in this country and different from what it is in America, at this season of the year.

29. For a month past, I send out every few days and buy half a pound of tobacco, and retail it

out, so that I can afford to sell better measure than can be bought at public market at the gate, and thus oblige myself and my neighbors.

30. To-day we had clothes served out to us, and some who were almost naked received a jacket, breeches, and two shirts, two pairs of stockings, a pair of shoes, and a cap. I received only a pair of shoes. Although I have been a prisoner more than twelve months, I have received only a pair of shoes from government; for we have reason to think that the clothes and bedding which were served to our company on board the Burford, were given us by the captain of the ship.

31. Those who did not receive clothes yesterday, had them to-day, except shoes, which they are to have in a few days; and those who petitioned the Board to go on board His Majesty's ships, received an answer from the Lord of the Admiralty, that all those who are legally committed to prison could not be bailed. However, our long-wished-for day draws near, for to-morrow the Act will expire, by which we were committed to prison. But we hear that it is likely to be renewed again; God forbid it should be so.

1778. January 1. I wish myself and all my brother fellow-sufferers a very happy new year. I do not know how to express my joy for so good a beginning, but by hoping that it will end better.

No sooner is this very impolitic Act out, than our friends make themselves known to us, which before they dared not do. To-day we had sent to us a plum pudding, and a sixpenny white loaf, to each mess, as a new year's gift, which, with our allowance, was sufficient for one day. Some gentlemen, also, who are friends, came to see us, and among the number was one Mr. Hancock, cousin of John Hancock, president of the Continental Congress. They inform us that upwards of £800 sterling have been raised in London for the relief of the prisoners here, and that they are daily raising more. They further told us, that we should not want for any thing, so long as we are prisoners in England. Transporting words! We have found friends in adversity. "Friends in need, are friends indeed."

2. To-day we received nothing but our usual allowance.

3. To-day we had sent to us a pound of soap to each man!

4. Sunday. We had sent to us a four pound loaf, and about six ounces of shag tobacco, to each mess, which we are told was given us by private gentlemen.

5. We had sent us a gallon of potatoes, to each mess, and oatmeal to thicken our broth.

6. To-day we had half a pint of peas instead of

greens, to each mess; by order from the Board, we are to have peas four times a week, which we like very much.   Again, also, we had a white loaf sent us to each mess, and a small number of books. To-day two boys, in prison, were tied up and whipped, a dozen each, for making game of the provision, because it was not cooked well.

7. To-day one hundred and fifty blankets were sent us, to be given to those who need them most ; and as there are two hundred and eighty-nine prisoners here, there is not one to each man ; so those who have the best bedding receive none, and as I have sufficient, I want none.

8. We had a threepenny loaf to each mess, sent us to-day, and as four of our number, who came last to prison, have not had the small-pox, they went to the hospital to be inoculated.

9. This afternoon a number of gentlemen came, and read a letter to us, which gives an account of upwards of £200 sterling having been raised in Bristol, for the relief of the prisoners here ; also, an account of £2,276 raised in London, for the same purpose.   In Portsmouth, we hear that there are about one hundred and forty prisoners, so that the number here and there, amounts to four hundred and twenty-nine.   What we have received hitherto, has no connection with these donations, but was given by private gentlemen.

10. We had sent us a threepenny loaf to each mess, and three hundred herring, to be divided amongst us. Also, it being a pleasant day, the prison was smoked with charcoal and brimstone, as is customary once in a few days.

11. We hear that Parliament is warned to meet six days sooner than it adjourned for.

12. To-day is the first that we have received any thing from the donation raised for us, and now we have a stated rule, which is a fourpenny loaf each day, out of the money raised in Bristol, except a few officers, who of choice, receive the money instead of bread. We hear no more as yet, of the money raised in London, but we suppose it is not come down.

13. We are told that ten recruiting parties are gone out into the country, from the regiment which guards us. Also, Captain Henry Johnston received a letter from his brother in London, wherein he desires him to make himself easy, for we shall all be exchanged in the spring.

14. To-day two ministers came to see us, and informed us of many good things preparing for us, which are too numerous to mention here; but if we receive them, I shall give an account of them hereafter.

15. It is fourteen months to-day, since we sailed from Newbury. Also, we had sent us to-day, a

yard of tobacco to each mess, and we are told that we are to have a yard every other day, which is four inches and a half to each man, per day.

16. Those who did not receive shoes on the 30th or 31st of last month, received them to-day. Also, we hear that all the wearing apparel that we have received as yet, was given us by government, but we are told that each of us is to have a great coat and a suit of clothes out of the money raised for us. Also, to-day we have another fourpenny loaf to each mess, which makes eight pennyworth of bread to each mess, per day, besides our allowance by government. We are advised by all our friends without, to make ourselves contented for a little while, for they tell us that they have all the reason in the world to believe that we shall be out of prison in three months. We had sent us a number of printed exhortations, urging us to lead a civil, sober life, and to leave off swearing and profaning the name of the Lord, for that is the last thing that many do before they sleep, and the first after they awake.

17. To-day we had clothes served out to us, out of the money raised for us; such as two shirts, two pairs of stockings, a pair of shoes, jacket and breeches, to those who needed them, and caps. The officers received white linen shirts instead of check, and hats instead of caps.   They tell us we

are all to have great coats in a few days; the clothes have not all come, so we are not all served. I was served to-day. I received two shirts, two pairs of stockings, a pair of shoes, a jacket and cap. We had also, a pound of pork to each mess, to eat with our peas; and we are told that we are to have it every Saturday. We had tobacco served again, and are told it is to be continued.

18. Sunday. We have an addition of about half a pound of beef to each mess.

Lord Cornwallis arrived yesterday in the Sound, from America. We hear that Howe has taken all the forts which command the Delaware.

19. Last night there was a heavy thunder-squall, and if I mistake not, there has been but one thunder-shower since I have been in England. Yesterday was the Queen's birth-day, but on account of its being Sunday they did not fire; but to-day each ship in commission, the fort and garison, fired twenty-one guns as a royal salute.

20. To-day they have again been serving clothes, but have not finished.

21. The remainder in prison had clothes served to them, so that each man in prison has received a great coat, and a suit, or nearly a suit, of clothes, out of the donation fund. We have, also, had our broth thickened, and it is to be continued; besides

a pound of beef to each mess more than our allowance by government.

22. We have now got into a settled rule of receiving our donation. The officers, such as captains and lieutenants, are allowed five shillings
a week ; sailing masters and prize masters, four
shillings a week ; boatswains, carpenters, and such
like, three shillings per week, and privateers-men,
two shillings per week, which is laid out in such
provisions as we think proper. What we receive
in provisions, besides the government allowance,
is as follows : one pound and a quarter of bread to
each mess, and a quarter of a pound of beef per
day, except Saturday; we then receive a quarter of
a pound of pork. We have thickening and leeks in
our broth; tobacco we receive every other day ;
soap we receive as we want it ; but the officers,
what they do not receive in provisions receive
in money. We have now every thing that we
want as to provisions and clothing ; but there is
one thing yet lacking — a thankful heart.

23. As keeping ourselves clean is conducive to
health, the agent has indulged us, for a few days
past, with liberty for six of us per day, to go down
into a separate yard to wash, where there is a
pump and convenience for washing.

24. I have heard little or no news, for this week

past, and indeed no news is the best news for us;
for if there is any thing against us, they are ready
enough to tell us.

25. Sunday. Cold, blustering, unsteady weather.

26. It is fourteen months to-day, since we sailed
from Portsmouth. To-day I went down into the
hospital yard to see one of my sick acquaintances,
who is down with the small-pox, under an excuse
to go to wash.

CHAPTER X.

JANUARY 27. We are informed by the man who
contracts for our tobacco, that it is very scarce,
and hard to be got for the money ; it is three shillings and sixpence per pound, which is one shilling
and twopence dearer than it was at Christmas.
The officers, in a separate prison, are allowed to
burn candles in the evening until gun-fire, which
is eight o'clock.

28. To-day some new washing troughs were
brought to prison for us to wash our clothes in,
and now we have plenty of clothes, soap, water

and tubs to wash in. In general, we are tolerably clean.

29. It being a pleasant day, the prison was again smoked. Concerning being released, we have no reason to think that those gentlemen who gave us encouragement intend to flatter us, as often the darkest hour of the night is just before day. It may be so with us, as those things which we have received since new year, came entirely unexpected to us; who knows but our redemption may come as suddenly and unexpectedly; so that I think it becomes us to put things on a medium, and make the best of a bad bargain; not to let our fears exceed our hopes, nor to put so much dependence on getting out, as to be disappointed of it; but as we are committed to prison by a civil magistrate for high treason, it is the opinion of some, that it is not in the power of the King or council to release us without some sort of a trial.

30. Yesterday afternoon, about sixty pairs of blankets were sent for those who had none. We also have the paper, wherein is an extract of a letter from a nobleman in the British service in America. He writes, that Cornwallis embarked on such a day, for home, to lay before the King and council the true state of America; he writes that the Americans want for nothing that is necessary, while they are in want of every thing.

Beef is four shillings per pound in Philadelphia, and other fresh provisions in proportion; and flour is not to be had. He states that it is wholly owing to Howe's good conduct that they are not totally cut off to a man, but if the Schuylkill freezes over, it is not too late to do it yet. We also have a paper, wherein is Lord North's proposition for reconciliation with America.

February 1. Sunday. Last evening, between seven and nine o'clock, five of the officers in a separate prison, who had agreed with the sentry to let them go, made their escape and took two sentries with them. The five officers were Captain Henry Johnston, Captain Eleazer Johnston, Offin Boardman, Samuel Treadwell and one Mr. Deal. Captain Henry Johnston having several suits of good clothes, he gave each sentry one, which they put on, and left their regimentals at their posts, with their firelocks, and made off; they were soon discovered by the guard, and pursued, but not taken.

3. I had a quantity of cedar brought to me to make boxes of.

4. This afternoon a fleet of about twelve or fifteen sail, with a convoy, arrived in the Sound, and saluted the admiral. It is thought they are part of Burgoyne's fleet, as we have heard that they were expected home.

5. To-day two large ships went from the Sound up to Ammoors, one of which had lost her main-top-mast. We are told that the three parties that went in pursuit of those who made their escape a few evenings ago, returned unsuccessful.

6. For two or three days I have been out of wood, so that I have done very little work, but to-day I had enough brought to last me a month.

7. To-day we had half a pound of pork more than usual, to each mess, which makes a pound and a half to each mess.

8. Sunday. We have the paper wherein is an extract of a letter from Dr. Franklin, Dean and Lee, to Lord North, and to the ministry, putting them in mind of the abuse which the prisoners have received from time to time, and giving them to know that it is in the power of the Americans to make ample retaliation, but they hoped that there was more humanity left in their hearts. They also wrote concerning an exchange of prisoners, and that if they would not exchange, they hoped that Congress would be permitted to appoint an agent to supply the prisoners in England with such things as were necessary, at their own expense. We learn that their answer was, that in America there was an exchange.

11. For some days past, the masons have been at work building a chimney.

12. We have a paper wherein is an account of
the House of Parliament being very full, and that
there is upwards of two hundred and fifty for car⁻
rying on the war, and upwards of one hundred and
fifty for settling it.   I am glad to find that the mi-
nority increases fast; the same paper informs us
that there is nearly one half against the method
they take in raising money to carry on the war,
and there is a disturbance about the method they
take for raising troops.   The same paper also informs us, that their troops at home are five
thousand six hundred and seventy-three short of
the peace establishment, and that there is only
about ten thousand troops in England, Ireland,
Scotland, Gibraltar and Mahon.

13. Many people in England, besides us prisoners, thought that Burgoyne's troops were to be
sent home, as we have heard, agreeably to their
capitulation, but by this time we are persuaded to
the contrary.

14. For two or three days I have been out
of wood, so that I have done but little work ; till
within a few days I have received three shillings
for boxes.

15. To-day it is fifteen months since we sailed
from Newbury.

16. To-day it snowed about three hours, just so

as to cover the ground. It is the first time the ground has been covered this winter.

17. Clear and cold. It is now we find the benefit of our great coats. We hear that the two soldiers that deserted and went off with the before-mentioned officers, from the prison, have been taken; which I am sorry to hear, for they will undoubtedly both be shot; and not only so, but I am afraid that their being taken will be followed with other bad consequences.

18. The chimney, in a separate prison, is so far completed, that we have a fire in it. To-day about twelve o'clock, the Governor of Plymouth and his lady, came to see us, and bought some of our wooden ware, and tasted of our broth; he said it was very fine, as indeed it has been, ever since we have had it thickened, and leeks put into it.

19. We are told by almost every one that comes to the gate, that a French war is near at hand, and cannot be avoided.

20. To-day each man in prison had a check linen handkerchief sent to him, which was given us by the donation. Also, to-day the officers in this prison moved into another, which has been preparing for them, so that all the officers who were committed to prison, as such, are in a prison by themselves.

21. Some time ago we had two fourpenny loaves

to each mess, per day, but one of them was soon taken off; and as they told us we should have as much provision as we wanted, we made it known to them, that we were desirous of having a sixpenny loaf instead of the fourpenny one, which they granted, and to-day we received a sixpenny loaf to each mess.

22. Sunday. We hear that General Gates sent a letter to one of the Parliament, in which he deplores the state of Great Britain, and advises them to make peace, before the Americans form alliance with any other nation. But he states that they will accept of nothing short of independence.

23. We have been informed several times, lately, that all the Acts since the year 1763, are likely to be repealed. "Peace with America and war with France," is the cry of almost every Briton. We have a paper in prison wherein is Lord North's speech in the House. He confesses that the English troops in America, have been beaten by inferior numbers. For several evenings past, we have had candles burning in prison, unknown to the agent, turnkey or guard; but I expect it will not be long before we shall be allowed to burn them, as we have written to the Board concerning it. We hear that a proclamation is issued for a public fast throughout England, Ireland and Scotland.

25. We hear that commissioners are appointed to go to America to treat with Congress; and they are to be considered a legal body while in treaty with them.

26. Last night the snow fell about two inches deep, on a level, which is more than it has snowed, put it all together, during the winter.

27. This day is kept as a public fast, throughout the united kingdom. I suppose they did not think it worth while to proclaim a fast before, as I do not remember that there has been one since I have been a prisoner, except a yearly fast. It is the opinion of many in prison, that if the proposals have not already gone to America, that we shall be sent with them, to give an assurance that they are real.

28. We are credibly informed that America has formed an alliance with France, for the space of twenty-one years; but whether it is any thing more than an alliance for trade, we have not yet learned. We hear that it took place the 26th of this month. We also hear that the money raised in England for the Americans here, amounted to £7000 sterling.

March 1. Wet, dirty weather, which obliges us to keep house most of the time. To-day is the first day of spring, and I have some secret expectations of being liberated before the season is ex-

pired, as there is a fleet of transports, with provision, bound to America, which will be ready to
sail by the last of this month, or the first of April.
Some think it probable that we may be sent with
them.

2. Warm and pleasant for the season.   We received an answer to the petition we wrote for the
liberty to burn candles in the evening, but the answer was that we could not be allowed the privilege.

3. We have a paper in prison, from which we
learn that Congress has made a present of a gold
medal to General Gates, and a sword to the com-
mander at Mud Island, for their bravery.   There
is also a slur upon Howe, in the paper, which is,
that he has got three miles in length, and two in
breadth, in the late campaign.

4. To-day, every man's clothing was examined to see if we keep ourselves clean.   Last evening one of the prisoners was sent to the Black-
hole, for abusive words spoken to the agent, and
another to-day, for selling his clothes, which were
given him, to get money to gamble with.

5. Remarkably pleasant weather for the season.
It is so warm, and the yard is so dry, that we all
carried our hammocks and bedding out to air.
Yesterday, Captain Lee received a letter, by the
way of Bilboa, from Newbury, from Mr. Tracy,

by which we learn tnat he is daily striving for our
exchange.

6. Although we are not allowed lights in prison,
yet we have them every evening, and intend
to till we are found out; and then they can do no
more than deny us of them, for when we cannot
get candles, we burn marrow-bones, which give a
very good light, and a good bone will last as long
as half a candle

CHAPTER XI

MARCH 7. We are told that the two soldiers
who deserted and carried five of the officers from
prison, on the evening of the 31st of January,
have had their trial. One of them is condemned
to be shot, the other to receive seven hundred
stripes. After their trial some handbills were
sent to the barrack, to the dock, and to Plymouth,
to set forth the heinousness of their crime in de-
serting their colors and carrying off rebels with
them; but the people in the King's dock-yard,
and some sailors who were on shore from the men-

of-war, gathered in a mob; got all the bills together that they could find, and burnt them.

8. Sunday. We hear that there has been several commissioners chosen to go to America, but they all refuse to go.

9. For the week past I have been something poorly, but the prisoners in general are remarkably healthy; never did I hear of such a number of men confined together who enjoyed such perfect health, and had so little sickness as we have. Even upon short allowance we enjoyed our health, though every man pined away to merely skin and bone. Those who had no money to help themselves, and looked pale and ghastly, and were so weak as scarcely to be able to walk, now look brisk, lively, and we all are strong, fat, and hearty.

10. We are informed that about three hundred merchants in London, Bristol and other places, have petitioned for peace with America, otherwise they will be entirely ruined. We hear that a great part of the merchants in Bristol are broken, and worth nothing.

11. We learn that some recruiting parties that went into Cornwall to obtain recruits, met with a very severe reception; the people gathered together and disarmed them, and drove them out of their territory. Indeed, all England seems to be

in commotion : it is the opinion of some, that should the American war continue another year, there would be civil war in England ; it seems to be but little short of it now.

12. We are informed that General Howe has written home for a reinforcement immediately, or he must inevitably share the fate of Burgoyne ; this inspires us with fresh courage. To-day our two fathers came to see us, as they commonly do once or twice a week. They are Mr. Heath and Mr. Sorry, the former is a Presbyterian minister, in Dock ; the latter a merchant in Plymouth. These are the two agents appointed by the committee in London to supply us with necessaries. A smile from them seems like a smile from a father; they tell us that every thing goes on well on our side, so that I hope our long wished for prize is just at hand — a prize that is preferable to any other earthly enjoyment. I hope our days of trouble are nearly at an end, and after we have borne them with a spirit of manly fortitude, we shall be returned to a free country to enjoy our just rights and privileges, for which we have been so long contending. This will make ample satisfaction for all our sufferings. To-day we received two shillings per mess, which is sixpence per man ; this is back money that we had not received, as we receive two shillings per man a week ; what

we do not receive in provisions we have in money.

13. Three Marblehead men came to see us, who were lately taken in a merchantman bound to France. They are about two months from America. They had the liberty to talk with us for nearly an hour. To-day three men were brought to prison, they being officers of a privateer that was taken and carried to the West Indies. They inform us that provisions are so scarce in the English islands that the inhabitants move from one island to another on that account, and are almost starved ; they also inform us that Mr. Samuel Treadwell is taken, and is now on board the Blenheim ; he is one of the five who went out on the 31st of June.

14. To day Mr. Treadwell was brought back to prison and put immediately in the Black-hole, where he is to lay forty days on half allowance. This afternoon, for the misbehavior of three or four persons, we were all confined in prison ; and it being a very pleasant afternoon, it aggravated many so that they ran fore and aft the prison screaming, and some cried murder, which alarmed the guard, and we were turned out, and the offenders delivered up and sent to the Black-hole, where they must lay until orders come from the Board to take them out.

15. Sunday. For some days past I have spent

most of my time in reading, and I can better com-
pose myself to it now than I could six months ago.

16. We are informed that on Saturday an
American privateer chased a merchantman into
the mouth of this harbor, and then hoisted her
colors and made the best of her way from land;
and that a frigate, that lay in the Sound, slipped
her cable and went after her.

17. St. Patrick's Day. By what we can learn,
a French and Spanish war is very near at hand.
The French are making all preparation for the
contest, so also are the English, for we are told
that all the ships belonging to the navy, that with
repairing will be fit for sea, are to be put in
commission immediately; and such a hot press as
there is now in England was never known — they
press against all protections.

18. To-day another was sent to the Black-hole,
for selling the clothes which were given to him;
which is no more than right. We are informed
that we are to be removed very soon and carried
to Chester castle, but we pay no regard to it; for
I believe two-thirds in prison expect to be sent to
America within three months.

19. We hear again that we are to be carried to
Chester, but pay no regard to it, as I said before.

20. We are informed that last night two or three
hundred men were pressed in Plymouth, and

Dock; even the lamp-lighter who tends the lamps about the prison, was pressed; but as he was in the King's service he was released. A lieutenant of one of the King's ships came to prison and advised those who had a mind to go on board the men-of-war to petition immediately. Accordingly a petition was written and signed by six old countrymen, and sent to the commissioners.

21. Dull, thick weather, some rain, so that we keep house.

22. Sunday. Some time ago we heard that some troops were to be sent to America this spring, but to-day we hear that their orders are countermanded.

23. To-day four or five large ships sailed from the Sound, bound to Spithead to join a fleet. We were found out to-day in conveying bread to the half allowance men in the Black-hole; so there is now a stop put to it.

24. Pleasant, for the season of the year. We received a letter from two of the officers that made their escape from prison on the 31st of January last; they inform us that they were taken up in London, and are now on board a guard ship in Portsmouth, waiting to come round.

25. We were informed that a few days ago a large ship accidentally ran down a French brig

in the Sound; eleven men were drowned, and her mainmast carried away.

26. Last evening the guards discovered our lights in the prison, so that I am afraid there will be a stop put to it.

27. There are many in prison who have sold all their clothes that were given them by subscription, to get a little money to gamble with, and buy strong beer; some of these have been found out, and justice is likely to be done them.

28. We hear that an American Captain, who has long been confined in prison, in London, petitioned for a trial, and was cleared and set at liberty. He then sued them for false imprisonment, but he was immediately apprehended and sent to Newgate. He again petitioned for a trial, was again tried, acquitted, and set at liberty, and went off.

29. Sunday. Stormy, so that we keep house, except when we go to draw our provisions.

30. We are informed that tobacco is 5s. a pound; at Christmas it was only 2s. 4d.

31. To-day I received the books which myself and another sent out to buy. These are the "Preceptor," in two volumes; the price of them was twelve shillings. The reason of its being so long after we sent out for them before we received them, was, they could not be bought in Plymouth, and the bookseller had to send to London for them.

April 1. To-day the two soldiers who went off with five officers, on the evening of the 31st of January last, received their punishment; one was shot, the other whipped; they belonged to the Light Infantry in the regiment.

2. Warm, and something pleasant, and the yard begins to be dry again, so that we can return to our former sports; these are ball and quoits, which exercise we make use of to circulate our blood and keep us from things that are worse.

3. This afternoon the agent and his clerk, the steward and doctor, seated themselves opposite the prison door and called over the roll, and ordered us one by one to pass out, and we were examined to see if we had our full compliment of clothing that was given us, and that they were clean and in order.

4. To-day each of us again received sixpence, which was back money, as before mentioned. Also, three of his Majesty's ships sailed — the Queen, of ninety guns, the Ocean, of ninety guns, both three-deckers, and the Fieutryant, a two-decker of eighty-four guns, which was taken from the French, the last war; we are told that she is the longest ship in the navy.

5. Sunday. It is ten months to-day since I came to prison. One Sunday passes away after another, seemingly disregarded by us, to our shame.

6. We keep house to-day on account of it being wet weather, and the prison yard is very muddy.

7. Mr.Heath, one of our fathers, has been in London, for near a month, and Mr. Sorry is to set out in a few days.   To-day the latter came to see us, and we desired him, for the future, to send us a fourpenny white loaf to each mess, per day, in place of a sixpenny one, for we have more provisions than many of us want to eat; and any person can easily conjecture that prisoners in our situation, who have suffered so much for the want of provisions, would abhor such an act as to waste what we have suffered so much the want of.

8. We are informed that the English ambassador has returned from France, and upon his return he inforned His Majesty that the King of France had recognized the independence of America.

9. Very warm and pleasant, so that all the prisoners in this prison carried their bedding out into the yard to air, and the prison was smoked with charcoal and sulphur, as is customary every few days.   To-day we received a fourpenny loaf according to our request.

10. To-day Captain Boardman and Mr. Deal were brought back to prison, which makes three of the number brought back who went out on the 31st of January last.   The other two were Captain Henry Johnston, of the Lexington, and Cap-

tain Eleazer Johnston, of the Dolton. These, we suppose, have got·clear. Also, this afternoon William Titcomb, a Newbury man, came to see us, about half an hour, and very glad was I to see him. He was taken in the Yankee Hero, by the Milford. He informs us that he has belonged to the Milford ever since he was taken, and he has been present at the capture of four American privateers. Upon their passage home, they took a vessel, which was one of the Civil Usage's prizes. The Milford arrived about three weeks ago. Titcomb has been unwell, and has been in the royal hospital most of the time since he arrived. He told us that he had rather be in our situation than his.

11. Very warm and pleasant; it is as warm as it was any time last summer. The spring is very forward, much more so than the last; but we were told that last spring was uncommonly backward.

12. Sunday. It is twelve months to-day since I set my foot upon this island, but now I think the auspicious day is about to dawn, when, if it is the Lord's will, we shall bid it farewell. To-day, by an order from the Board, we drew cabbage instead of broth, and we are to have cabbage two days in a week, peas two, and broth three, which we like much better; for when a person is confined to one steady diet, and has enough, he soon gets tired of it.

13. We are informed by Captain Boardman,
that while he was out, he saw one Mr. Bapson,
lately from America, who belonged to Cape Ann.
He informed him that a new ship of twenty-six
guns, which was built by the Marine Society of
Newbury, Captain William Friend, master, just
after she got over the Bar, filled and sunk, and a
number of men were drowned.   He also informs
us that Captain James Tracy in the new ship Hero, has not been heard of since he sailed; and
that the schooner Washington has been absent
some months, and they are afraid she is lost. William Titcomb, who was here a few days ago, told
us that Tracy, in company with another frigate,
was cruising off the Cape of Good Hope.

14. We are informed that Governor Johnston
and two others, have kissed His Majesty's hand,
and are appointed commissioners to go to America.

15. What money I have received for boxes since
I have been in prison, amounts to over three guineas.   Had it not been for this money, I must inevitably have suffered more than I did.

16. Very warm and pleasant; the grass and
herbs in the fields appear to us as forward, from
what we can see from the prison, as they do the
first of June in America.

CHAPTER XII.

APRIL 17. To-day one of the prisoners received a letter from Captain Harris, of Portsmouth. He writes that we may rely upon it, that he had it from good authority, that the vessels were taken up, and were under repairs, to carry us home ; and according to his letter, he expects to be on his passage in a month's time. There are many in prison who gather some encouragement from this.

18. According to the best accounts, there has been a great debate in the House of Commons.— The Duke of Richmond is for giving the Commis-

sioners full power, before they return, even to declare the States independent, if nothing short will
answer; Mr. Fox and Mr. Burke are of the same
mind. But Lord Chatham declares that he had
rather be in his grave than see the day that Amer-
ca is declared to be independent. According to
their own account, this American war has cost
Great Britain £30,000,000, and thirty thousand of
their best disciplined troops — eleven thousand
eight hundred the last campaign.

19. We are informed that a packet has lately
arrived from America, but as yet we know not
what news she has brought.

20. We have a paper in which is an account of
twenty-eight sail of vessels, laden with English
goods, laying in some port of England, bound to
America.

21. We have accounts in the paper of the Boston frigate, and another frigate out of Boston, having taken a number of valuable prizes.

22. There was one man came from the Black-
hole, his time being up. There are four more
left therein, but we find means to help them, as we
have others before them; we having a plenty of
provisions, can help them, and not injure ourselves.
To-day I went out to buy a small pocket Bible,
the price of which was three shillings and sixpence.

24. Three more came out of the Black-hole; there is but one left, and he will be out in a few days.

25. Captain Lee received a letter from Captain Trott, a prisoner in Bristol. He wrote that those of us who have a mind to write to America, can do so, by immediately sending the letters to him. He will send them to France by a man bound there. Several, therefore, wrote, and sent them to him. He also informed us, that by his own desire, he is going to London to receive his trial, which put us in mind of petitioning for a trial, also. Accordingly, a petition was drawn up, and about one half in prison signed it. The contents of the petition were as follows:

" To the King's Most Excellent Majesty: the petition of sundry of the subjects of the United States of America, showeth, that your petitioners were at several respective periods, in the year of our Lord 1777, committed to Old Mill Prison, in the County of Devonshire, for the suspected crime of high treason; your petitioners are unable to be exactly positive as to the particular style or wording of the crime represented, in whole or either of their commitments, but as their bodily health is at present much impaired, and they fear it will be more so, so that their lives may be endangered by a longer confinement in prison, they humbly request that your Majesty will be pleased to order them to be brought to trial with all possible speed, for the crime or crimes of which they may be supposed guilty. And your petitioners," &c.

26. For some months past we have thought it presumption to try to make our escape from prison by digging out, on account of there being traitors amongst us. An innocent man has borne the scandal of this a good while, but upon being told of it by a friend, he took no rest day or night until he had found the traitors, and upon examination we discovered them to be two negroes, a man and a boy. Accordingly, they were tied up and whipped — the boy was whipped by a boy, two dozen and a half lashes, on his bare back ; and we thought it the man's prerogative who had borne the blame of being a traitor and was innocent, to lay the stripes upon the negro man. Accordingly, he gave him three dozen upon his bare back, and spared not; had the negro stayed till night he would have left his ears ; but I suppose that he was suspicious of that, so he went and jumped over the gate and delivered himself up to the guard and told his story. The negro boy was sent for ; so now they are both separated from us in another yard, and it is well for them that they are so.

27. A man came out of the Black-hole, his time being up, and Mr. Boardman and Deal, who have

been only seventeen days on half allowance in the prison hospital, were sent into this yard. They are the only persons who have broke out and been taken, who have not suffered forty days on half allowance in the Black-hole.

28. Last evening being somewhat dark, two young men had a mind to try to make their escape; one of whom cut his hammock and blanket into strips and tied them together; got over the wall at the end of the prison into the yard, and was there caught and sent to the Black-hole. To-day all the negroes were taken out of this prison, and put into a separate building, called the itchy yard.

29. To-day is Wednesday, which is our pay day, and each man received sixpence; and as we have received it regularly for some weeks past, we are told that we are to have it weekly; so in future, I shall only mention when we do not have it.

30. There is a number sick now, more than has been since we came to prison, except in time of small-pox. There are three or four in the prison hospital who are very sick with fever, and several more in this prison who are very ill. For a few weeks past, the agent has indulged us with the liberty of pens, ink and paper, so that we have an opportunity for writing and cyphering.

May 1. To-day the Tarbay, a ship of seventy-

four guns, as she lay at her moorings, accidentally took fire, and we are told that her upper works
are burned to a coal, and being old, she is not
worth repairing; she has been but a few days out
of dock.

3. We have a newspaper, from which we learn
that an American privateer, commanded by Captain John Paul Jones, from Portsmouth, went into
Whitehaven, sent her boat on shore, and spiked
up the cannon, and set fire to a ship, and had it
not been for a man that deserted the boat and
alarmed the town, the boat's crew would have set
fire to all the shipping in the harbor. They then set
off and went to Scotland, where they went on shore
and plundered Lord Selkirk's house of £5000 worth
of plate, and took several cattle. To-day a large
ship arrived in the Sound, which we took to be an
East Indiaman, but have since heard that she is a
transport from New York.

3. Sunday. To-day we received two letters
from the prisoners in Portsmouth. They inform
us that there are one hundred and eighty prisoners
there. They also inform us that Captain Weeks,
in a privateer of sixteen guns, bound from France
to America, foundered upon the Banks of Newfoundland, and all were lost but one.

4. To-day, Captain Lee, taken in a merchantman belonging to Manchester, came to see us. He

informed us of Captain Tracy's arrival, and that
he had taken an East Indiaman ; but we do not
hear of any homeward bound East Indiamen missing.

5. To-day several of us had an opportunity of
writing letters to send by Captain Lee, who came
to see us yesterday, as he is bound directly home.

6. This morning about eight o'clock, Mr. John
Fowler, a prisoner, died in the prison hospital,
with a pleurisy fever. He was only a few days
sick, and in the afternoon there was a jury over
him. They will not tell us the occasion of a jury's being called, but it appears that the public
were jealous that there had been bad usage. This
man is the fourth that has died since I came to
prison. He is the first of Captain Lee's men that
has died since they were imprisoned.

7. To-day there have been several men drunk in
prison, as there often is when they can get money
to buy beer; and there has been a wrangle between the old countrymen and the Americans.
The Americans unanimously hang together, and
endeavor to keep peace in prison, but if the former
party were stronger than the latter, we should have
a hell upon earth.

8. This afternoon there were three prisoners
brought to prison, who were taken in a prize upon
the Grand Bank, bound to America, by a large old

East Indiaman, which has been made a transport.
She was bound from New York to England, with
a few of Burgoyne's officers on board, wounded
and exchanged.   The three who came to prison
tell us that they had the offer of entering the English service, yet they chose to come to prison.
The prize-master's mate entered the service; of
those who came to prison, there was one Newbury
man, one Casco Bay man, and one Philadelphia
man.

9. To-day three large two deckers dropped
down into the Sound, from Ammoors, bound to
Spithead, to join the fleet that is bound to sea, for
the purpose of watching the motions of the French.

10. The commissioners sailed from Portsmouth
in the Trydant man-of-war, of sixty-four guns,
bound for America, April 22d.

11. We have a hole now in hand, and as we
have not convenient places in prison to conceal all
the dirt, for many days past many of us have been
employed in the smuggling way, by carrying it out
in our pockets and under our great coats, and emp-
tying it into the vaults; but this afternoon we met
with a misfortune, for a hole which we had been
digging for ten days past, by times, foundered.

12. This morning after we were turned out, we
so contrived it that the officer should enter into
conversation with the turnkey and sentry on guard,

and draw their attention, and in the meantime we stopped the hole, so that it was not discovered.

13 We are resolved to be in the way of our duty, by embracing every opportunity to make our escape.

14. To-day about one o'clock, another prisoner died in the prison hospital. It is thought that he died of consumption. His name was Joseph Kensington; he was taken in the Lexington privateer, with Captain Henry Johnson. He is the fifth man that has died since we came to prison. If a man is ever so sick in prison, he has nothing allowed him by the doctor that is nourishing, but a little barley-water and milk broth; but we have reason to think that all necessary things are allowed by government, but it is left to the doctor's option; so the sick do not have them at all.

15. It is eighteen months to-day since we sailed from Newbury, but I hope in a few months to be exchanged; and I expect that matters will be settled amicably, for it is the opinion of many people that come to the gate to see us, and of a great part in prison, that the commissioners are invested with full power to settle the difficulties before they return, upon the best terms; even to declare the States independent, if necessary.

CHAPTER XIII.

MAY 16. We are informed that a French privateer was taken by a Guernsey privateer, a few days
ago, and brought in here. She had eighty men on
board, a number of whom were officers. bound
to America. We are informed that she had
a commission to sink, burn and destroy all
that she met belonging to Great Britain. We have
also a newspaper, by which we learn that a French
fleet, consisting of twelve sail of the line, and six
frigates, sailed from Toulon on the 13th of April,
and passed through the Straits of Gibraltar on the

24th, commanded by Count D' Estaing, supposed to be bound to America.

17. Sunday. We are informed by the paper, that on the 10th of this month, William Pitt died. I think that all England has reason to mourn the loss of so great a man, at this critical juncture, and the house of Bourbon to rejoice.

18. Mr. Sorrey, one of our "fathers," has returned from London. He informs us that General Burgoyne had arrived in London before he left, but whether he is exchanged, or come home on parole, we have not yet learned. Mr. Sorrey tells us that we must exercise a little more patience. We cannot, however, gather much patience in the yard, it is rather inclined to nettles.

19. We hear that General Burgoyne came home on parole of honor, and is to return as soon as he has dispatched his business.

20. To-day Mr. Walch, one of the lieutenants of the Lexington, about two o'clock in the afternoon, had an invitation from a sentry that stood without the wall at one corner of the yard, to go out. Accordingly he dressed himself, and went as directed. At night, when the guard came to turn them into the prison, it was so contrived that a small boy should go in first, and then slip out of a window and be counted in twice ; so that they had their number and did not miss him.

21. This morning when they were turned out they did the same, and by that means it was not found out. This contrivance was to screen the guard that was on duty, when he went out, fearing lest if it was found out, they would mistrust which way he escaped, and thus the sentry be exposed.

22. Last night, the second time the guard went into the officers' ward, they found that one of them was missing ; but it was about thirty hours after he went away, before they had the least suspicion of it. This morning, after we were turned out, we were mustered to see if there were any more gone, and while they were mustering us, one of the prisoners, with red hair, said something to the officer that he did not like, for which he threatened to put him in the Black-hole. After muster, accordingly, they made search for him, but could not find him, as they had no other mark for him but his hair. They then sent us into prison, and took aside each one that had red hair, but they could not find him among the number, so they let the matter pass. This afternoon, another man got over the wall at the corner of the yard, by the vault, and, by his own folly, was taken and sent to the Black-hole. On account of this futile attempt, we were sent into the prison in the midst of a pleasant afternoon; and as they were turning us in, there was one man a little obstinate, who would

not voluntarily go in; they therefore took him to the Black-hole also.

23. This forenoon, as some of the prisoners were playing at ball in the prison yard, the ball happened to lodge in a spout that is placed under the eves of the prison to convey the water, when it rains, into the well in the yard. They sent a boy up after it, and one of the sentries without the wall saw him, levelled his gun at him and fired, but the ball happened not to touch him. To-day Admiral Biron and his fleet arrived in Plymouth Sound, from Spithead. The fleet consists of thirteen sail of the line, and one frigate. They are bound to America, in search of the French fleet that sailed from Toulon.

24. Sunday. For two days past, the guard has been so strict with us that they have placed a sentry at the gate, and do not allow a prisoner to go near it upon any occasion whatever; and this afternoon after we were turned into prison, one of the prisoners got up to a window to look out, and a sentry without, saw him and bade him get down; as he did not get down as soon as asked, he fired at him, but did not hurt him. We think the occasion of the guard's being so strict with us lately, is the conduct of a few evil-minded men in prison, who, as regularly as they receive their sixpence per week, lay it out at the gate for strong beer

— drink it all at once, and so get drunk. Then they abuse any one who comes across them.

25. We hear that the King has granted all the men in the fleet, that now lay in the Sound, eight days to frolic and make themselves merry.

26. To-day a poor American widow came to see us; she is daughter to Dr. Murray, in Newtown Chester, Maryland. She told us that she was lately from America, that her husband is dead, and she is left with three small children in a strange land, and with nothing to help herself. I do not know what business she had here, but as there were some who knew her in America, and as she seemed to be an object of charity, we contributed among us about a guinea, and gave it to her.

27. This morning, very early, the guard came in and surprised some of us, while we had a piece of the wall down, and were digging. Some one must go to the Black-hole for it, but as yet there is nothing done about it.

28. We hear that night before last, all the Fishermen in the harbor were pressed out of their fishing boats, on board of the fleet which now lays in the Sound.

29. To-day is what they call Royal Oak, or King Charles' restoration day, and each ship, fort, and garrison, fires a salute.

30. To-day another hole was begun.

31. This forenoon we were all turned out into the yard, but a few who stayed in to dig : and while they were at work, the guard happened to come in to drive a prisoner down from an end window; so they went directly up stairs, which gave those who were at work an opportunity of making off into the yard. But the guard, before they went out, found out the hole, and the agent declared that he would have four men go to the Black-hole, or the whole should be put on half allowance. He gave us until four o'clock in the afternoon to consider of it, and at the time four men delivered themselves up of their own accord, to go to the Black-hole, rather than that all should suffer. But as we are all equally concerned in every such scheme, satisfaction will be made to them by us.

This afternoon, one Captain Pulford, came to see us. He is only about forty days from North Carolina, and was taken in a merchantman bound to France. He informed us that General Lee has been exchanged.

June 1. Two gentlemen who came to see us to-day, informed us that the French Admiral, now laying in Brest with thirty-six sail of the line, besides frigates, sent a challenge to the English Admiral to meet him off Brest. We are also informed that there are orders from London for a larger prison, three stories high, separate, and in another yard, to be repaired for the reception of the French prisoners.

2. In expectation of some making their escape, a difficult piece of work was undertaken, which I hope we shall prosper in.

3. Ever since I have been in prison there have been vaults dug in the yard, for the prison offal, until within a fortnight. The vaults having since then been full, each man has taken his turn to empty the tubs, twice a day, into the river. This morning two in the Black-hole went to empty their tubs at the river's edge, about twenty-rods distant, and having a mind to try to make their escape, although part of the guard was with them, they left their tubs and ran. They were immediately pursued by the guard, and overtaken about a quarter of a mile distant; and after they were secured, they used them shamefully, knocking them down two or three times, and very badly injuring them. As our cook, who prepares our victuals, gave chase and caught one of them, we determined that he should suffer for it. This same cook has lately got a license to sell strong beer, and his wife tends daily at the gate, and there are many in prison who have bought of her a great deal. But we are unanimously agreed to buy no more of him. A man who has been only two days out of the

Black-hole, was carried there again to-day, for abusing the sentry in the yard.

4. To-day is the King's birth-day, and each ship, fort, and garrison, fired twenty-one guns as a royal salute. I think that his subjects would have more reason to rejoice at his death than at his birth-day; for according to the best accounts, the national debt is more than one hundred and forty-six millions. A commissioner has been here to-day, reviewing the prisons; I suppose to give orders in what manner they shall be repaired for the accommodation of the French. There are two of our ship's company that have been very ill for some months past, and as the doctor will not let them have things necessary for their comfort, we think it our duty to contribute to their relief, as Providence has put something in our hands. Accordingly, to-day we raised among us a trifle of money to buy them such things as they want, and we shall raise more as they need it. This afternoon, there were thirteen prisoners brought to prison from the Blenheim. They were lately brought from Liverpool, and have been taken nearly five months; they were captured in a privateer, fitted out of Salem. The captain's name is Ravel. To-day a fleet of fishermen, consisting of about thirty sail, went out of the Sound, bound to Newfoundland.

5. The fleet that sailed yesterday for Newfound-land, meeting with contrary winds, and the weather looking likely for a storm, put about and came in again. It is twelve months to-day since I came to prison. I believe four months ago it was the opinion of every one within these walls, that we should be out before this day, but I believe now, most of us despair of being exchanged this summer, unless General Burgoyne's coming home should be of advantage to us. He is able to represent the case as it is, for we hear that the Congress told him, before he left America, to go home and take his seat in Parliament, and speak the truth, for the truth could not hurt them.

> Twelve months in prison we have spent, —
> This judgment for our sins was sent,
> To awake us from our carnal sleep,
> And teach us God's commands to keep.

6. There are now four prisoners, who are sail-makers, at work in this prison, making hammocks for more prisoners. They are employed by a sail-maker without, and are allowed a trifle for their labor.

CHAPTER XIV.

JUNE 7. Sunday. This morning we are informed that our chief doctor is dead. He died very suddenly; I believe there are not many in prison who will mourn, as we have no reason to expect that we can get a worse one. This forenoon, after we were turned out, two men of this prison got into a drain at one corner of the yard, and were digging, when one of the turnkeys present found out that they were at work, and alarmed the guard. They were taken and carried

12

to the Black-hole, but we shall find means to help
them, as we have done others before. The hole
in which they were at work was commenced five
days ago. They had nearly finished the work before it was found out. Thus every method we take
to make our escape is found out before it is accom-
plished, and our unhappy efforts are not blest.

8. We hear that the fleet of men-of-war, now
lying in the Sound, have received orders for sailing; also, that the convoy of the Newfoundland
fleet, while they were out, took a sloop from North
Carolina, loaded with indigo, bound to France.

9. This morning the fleet sailed, under the
command of Admiral Biron; it consists of eleven
sail of the line, and two frigates. They are bound
in search of the French fleet, commanded by
Count de Estaing, which sailed from Toulon,
bound to America. To-day Captain Dennis, from
Cape Ann, came to see us; he was taken in a
brig out of Newbury. He informs us that Captain Tracy is wholly given over, which I am very
sorry to hear. Captain Dennis has got his clearance, and is bound directly home, and will carry
letters for those who desire to send. This afternoon thirteen more prisoners came to prison from
the ships; they belonged to the same privateer
with those who came last Thursday. For my
own part, I think it very poor encouragement for

us to see the number of prisoners increase; I think it looks very melancholy within these walls, and more and more so every day. I am so uneasy that I cannot content myself to do any thing; let me seem to be ever so busy, my mind is not fixed upon what I am about. It is dwelling upon my situation and condition.

10. To-day several of us wrote letters to send to America by Captain Dennis, but he has not yet come after them. When Mr. Sorrey came to bring us our money, he told us that orders were come for us to be exchanged for the prisoners in France. We put more confidence in what he says, because he has been very cautious hitherto of telling us news. To-day the whole prison has been in an uproar, occasioned by one or two drunken fellows, who, as regularly as they get any money, get drunk with the beer which is bought at the gate. One of these was so outrageous that he drew his knife, and walked fore and aft the prison, striking and abusing those he met. When we were turned out in the afternoon we complained to the agent, and he, by a desire of most of the men in prison, was sent to the Black-hole. After we delivered him up, he, out of spite, told of a window where some one in prison had sawed off a bar.

11. The commissioner has again been in the yard to talk with us.

12. To-day the fleet of Newfoundland fishermen sailed again, and I am afraid Captain Dennis has gone and left our letters.

13. There are now several masons and carpenters at work on an old three story prison, in another yard, repairing it for the reception of French prisoners. The man who was delivered up to the agent, a few days ago, is put in irons. He is the only one that has been put in irons since we came to prison.

14. The Rev. Mr. Heath has returned home from London, having been gone nearly three months; and yesterday afternoon he came to see us. He tells us that he has been informed that many of us pay no regard for the Sabbath, which is too true; for it is equally the same with many in this prison, whether it be the Sabbath or any other day. They will run about the yard, and play, and curse, and swear, and blaspheme, the greater part of the time. Many of them are the most wicked and profane men that I ever saw or heard of; but there are a great number of steady men. Mr. Heath gave us a few books, and he says that he has a number more to give to such as will make good use of them.

15. We hear that the reconciliation bill, which was sent to America from England, last February, met with a very cool reception, both by the American and Howe's troops, and was even treated with the greatest indignation by both. General Howe, we hear, is expected home soon, and General Clinton is to take the command at Philadelphia. We hear that there is now a Spanish fleet of twenty one sail of the line riding at anchor in Cadez, ready for sea. We have also heard it reported of late, that the American army is so destitute of clothing that they are obliged to strip the women of their petticoats to cover them. These things are put in the papers to amuse the public; but we know better; it is inconsistent with reason, and utterly false.

16. To-day we received a letter from one Captain Harris in Portsmouth prison; he writes to us that there are two hundred and fifty prisoners in France, and that we may depend upon it, that he had it from good authority, that we are to be exchanged for them, as far as they will go. But in this prison we are very faithless; we have been flattered too long for our profit. I heard some days ago that there were six hundred prisoners in France. There are now in these prisons three hundred and sixteen American prisoners.

. 17. We hear that Parliament is prorogued until

the middle of July.   I suppose by that time they expect to hear from the commissioners.

18. Yesterday, after we were turned out and the doors shut, three small boys entered through the grates into the prison and damaged several hammocks, for which, this morning, their ship's company tied them up and whipped them.   To-day four men came out of the Black-hole, who went in on the 31st of May; they have been in only eighteen days; the reason of their not tarrying longer is, a commissioner being here from London, they petitioned him for pardon, and he granted it.   There are only three left in the Black-hole now.

19. I hear, privately, that the soldiers have orders not to fire on the prisoners if they see any making their escape; to fire only clear powder to alarm the guard; and they are not to strike any of us, nor offer a bayonet to us: thus their rigor has been abated since Burgoyne has been taken.

20. This forenoon, Rev. Mr. Heath came and delivered us a letter, which we found to be from a gentleman who is one of the committee of appropriation for the money raised by subscription for the relief of American prisoners in this country. He desired that we should send him the name, former residence, and occupation, of all the prisoners; he assures us that there is a prospect of an ex-

change for some, if not all of us; he also desired
that we should keep good order, and by no means
attempt to elope. I lack words to express my
gratitude to these gentlemen; for had it not been
for our numerous friends, doubtless many of us
had now been in our graves.

21. Sunday. Notwithstanding our friend's ad-
vice, we have a plan in agitation for making our
escape, and are resolved to go on with it. Our
design is to get into a drain at the corner of the
yard, where the last hole was found out, and dig
up on the other side of the wall. For this purpose, yesterday afternoon three men took down a
piece of wall under a window, in an old prison
adjoining this drain. These men got into the
prison and the wall was put up again, and plas-
tered up with dirt. They dug into the drain and
tarried there all night and till after we were let
out in the morning, when we let them out. Last
night, when we were counted into prison, three
boys went in first and got out at the window, and
were counted twice, to make up the number.

22. Last night and to-day this scheme was carried on as before. This afternoon Captain Dennis and Captain Talford came and took our letters.
They have got their clearance and are bound directly to France. I sent a letter by Captain D.
to my father. Captain Dennis' hands consisted

of nine Beverly men; they are all kept on board
the men-of-war, as they have served all others during the war taken in merchantmen, except the
captains, and them they clear.

23. Last night the scheme was carried on the
same as before, till about 8 o'clock in the evening,
when they were discovered by the guard and sent
to the Black-hole; after which they went into the
officers' prison, where were Captain Bunten and
Captain Boardman walking; they were ordered
to bed, and they refused to go, for which they carried them to the Black-hole.   This afternoon one
of the prisoners was sent down to the prison hospital; he had been so sick and weak for some days
past, that when we were turned out into the yard,
and the door locked, (they having driven him out,)
as he could not walk, we were obliged to lead
him.   When out, he could not stand, but was
forced to lay down on the ground; and when
down, could not rise up without help.

24. Last night, there were two more carried to
the Black-hole from the officers' prison, for not being in bed when the guard came in, which was
between nine and ten o'clock.   The officers in
prison have drawn up a petition to send to the
board, to know if Mr. Coudry, the prison keeper,
has orders to confine any one for not being in
hammock at nine or ten o'clock in the evening.

25. According to the newspapers, General
Burgoyne gives the American troops a brave
name ; he says that the troops he had at his command were as good as double the number of any
other troops the King has, and that the American
troops were as good as his, and would fight as
well.

26. Yesterday afternoon, while the guard was
turning us into prison, four that were in the
Black-hole, and one that was in the hospital, broke
out through the drain, and got a boat a quarter of
a mile off, but they were soon discovered, and
pursued by the guard. The militia were raised,
and they were all taken in about half an hour and
brought back. This afternoon, those five, with
all the rest, were sent up into this yard. Those
who came to prison last had clothes given them,
which were allowed by government. I received
a pair of breeches, as I had not received any before since I came to prison. This morning a
French cutter was brought in here, taken by an
English cutter; and at the same time two French
frigates were taken, which, I hear, have arrived in
Portsmouth. Six of the wounded Frenchmen
were brought from the cutter to prison, and put
in the hospital.

27. This afternoon two of the officers in prison
had an invitation by a sentry to go over the wall,

which they did, but were discovered, taken, and
sent to the Black-hole.

28. We hear that the Arathusa frigate was dismasted in the engagement with the two French
frigates above mentioned.

29. Joseph Barnum, one of our company, who
has been unwell ever since he had the small-pox,
more than twelve months ago, has now got the
white swelling in his knee, which the doctor thinks
will occasion his death, if not cut off; and he is so
weak that I fear he is not able to undergo the
operation.

30. For a long time we have been imposed upon by the agent and butcher, by sending us bad
meat. Yesterday there were maggots found in
our beef, and we told the two butchers who go into the cook-room to inspect our meat — that if it
was the same to-day as yesterday, not to cut it up.
Accordingly, they went out this morning, and as
the meat proved to be very poor, our butchers refused to cut it up. Upon this, the agent ordered
the cook to cut it up, which he did, and cooked it.
At twelve o'clock the meat was brought in, in a tub;
but we had all agreed not to take any of it. The
agent told us if we would accept of it to-day, as
it was cooked, we should have no more like it,
but have better in future. He has, however, told
us these stories too often, and we thought if we

took it to-day, we should have the same another
day ; therefore we positively refused it ; for we
can live as well upon the fat that we have gathered
from the donation, two days, as we could seven
months ago upon all our allowance.

July 1. Last night six men in this prison attempted to make their escape ; they got out at a
window into the yard, but as they were trying to
get over the wall, they were discovered by a sentry, so they returned and got in at the window
where they got out.

2. To-day forty-seven more French prisoners
were brought to prison, but they were all foremast
hands ; for all the French officers are allowed to
go on parole. To-day the New Duke, a ship of
ninety guns, dropped down in the Sound, in order
for sailing. She is a new ship, and has been
launched since I came to prison.

3. As it is two years to-morrow since the
Declaration of Independence in America, we are
resolved, although we are prisoners, to bear it in
remembrance ; and for that end, several of us
have employed ourselves to-day in making cock-
ades. They were drawn on a piece of paper, cut
in the form of a half-moon, with the thirteen
stripes, a Union, and thirteen stars, painted out,
and upon the top is printed in large capital letters,

"Independence," and at the bottom "Liberty or Death," or some appeal to Heaven.

4. This morning when we were let out, we all hoisted the American flag upon our hats, except about five or six, who did not choose to wear them. The agent, seeing us all with those papers on our hats, asked for one to look at, which was sent him, and it happened to be one which had "Independence" written upon the top, and at the bottom, "Liberty or Death." He, not knowing the meaning of it, and thinking we were going to force the guard, directly ordered a double sentry at the gate. Nothing happened till one o'clock; we then drew up in thirteen divisions, and each division gave three cheers, till it came to the last, when we all cheered together, all of which was conducted with the greatest regularity. We kept our colors hoisted till sunset, and then took them down.

5. The carpenters and masons have been at work for some days past, repairing an old prison in the yard.

8. This afternoon, Rev. Mr. Heath came to see us, and gave us several books; he informs us that General Howe has arrived home, and that the King's troops have left Philadelphia.

9. We are told that Captain Dennis and Captain Talford, with five or six other American captains,

bought a small vessel to carry them to France, and yesterday morning set sail.

10. To-day Joseph Barnum, one of our company, and one of the French prisoners that was wounded, had their thighs cut off. Barnum has been unwell more than a year; he has had a white swelling in his knee.

11. We have a hole now in hand, which we thought this afternoon was found out, but it happened to be one within a few feet of it, which was discovered some time ago, and was of no great consequence.

12. Sunday. To-day Captain Lee received a letter from Portsmouth prison, from Jonn Dame, a Newbury man. He informs us that he was taken with Captain Dennis in a new privateer brig, of sixteen guns, that sailed from Boston on the 25th of May. On the 30th of the same month he was taken by the same frigate that General Howe came home in.

13. Since the Frenchmen came to prison we have been of considerable help to them, as we have now plenty of provisions, and many of us more than we want to eat. What we have to spare we give to them, and we daily give them more or less. Their allowance of bread is six pounds to four of them per day, which is one and a half pounds per man; but we rebels are allowed

only one pound of bread a man, per day, from
government.   The other allowances of the French
is the same as ours.

14. Admiral Keppel has lately sailed from St.
Helena with about twenty-eight sail of the line
and six frigates; and a French fleet has sailed from
Brest; but I cannot learn the exact number of
ships of which the fleet consists.   It is expected,
whenever these two fleets meet, there will be a
bloody engagement, for England's chief dependence is in her fleet.

15. It is twenty months to-day since I left Newbury.   To-day Admiral Keppel's fleet was seen
from the prison to pass by this harbor, and it is
expected that two or three ships from this port
will join them.   This afternoon four boys tried to
make their escape; they got over the wall into
the Frenchmen's yard, and hid in their hammocks,
but were soon discovered, and taken.

16. We hear that Parliament is prorogued until
some time in September next.   To-day the Sud-
bury, a ship of seventy-four guns, sailed to join
Admiral Keppel's fleet, which now appears off
this port.   The guard now consists partly of the
Cornish, partly of the Somersetshire, and partly
of the Devonshire militia, and some of the thir-
teenth regiment, which is the regiment that has
guarded us ever since we came to prison.

CHAPTER XV.

JULY 17. There are a number of very quarrelsome, lawless men in prison, who have been the occasion of a great deal of mutiny and disturbance amongst us, which has obtained for us the ill-will of our friends; and we have been informed that unless there is an alteration among us, our donations will be stopped; so that we thought it proper to have Articles among ourselves. These were drawn up to-day; they forbid all gambling, and blackguarding, which have caused great distur-

bance in the yard, and occasioned much fighting.
They also forbid any improper language to any officer or soldier, who are now, or may hereafter be,
appointed to preside over us.   These articles were
read in the yard before all the prisoners, and then
stuck up in prison, and two men out of each ship's
company were appointed to see them put into execution.

18. We hear that Count D' Estaing's fleet has arrived in Boston.   I learn, also, by the papers, that
twenty-five sail of the line are now laying at single
anchor in Cadiz, ready for sea.   Their place of
destination is not known.

19. Sunday.   As there have been many books
given in lately, the prison is much stiller of Sunday than formerly, and the people are much better
employed. This forenoon, as some were in a drain
digging, they were heard by the guard, but they
got out before the guard reached the hole.

20. Wet, rainy weather, so that we kept house
most of the day.   There has been little or no rain,
for two months, until last night and to-day.   The
ground has been so parched for want of rain, that
the fields look like the fall of the year.

21. Last night about nine o'clock, it being very
dark and rainy, we opened a hole at the back side
of the prison, large enough for two men to go out
abreast.   This hole has been ready for some time

past — they have only been waiting for a dark, stormy night; when they broke ground, the pavement fell in, and four men jumped out and got off. A sentry within ten feet of the hole, saw them, and immediately alarmed the guard; so that no more could escape. The guard came in, and while they were in prison the guard-house chimney took fire; upon which the drum beat to arms, and fire was cried. The cry was that the prisons were on fire, and the prisoners were breaking out. After this was over, the guard came in again and took nine of the prisoners and put them in the Black-hole, because they were up and had their clothes on. To-day, about one o'clock, four of the officers from the officers' prison got over the wall into the hospital yard; two of whom got out, but were soon discovered and taken. The other two were taken in the yard, and all put into the Black-hole last night, but came out to-day.

22. Yesterday noon, another hole was begun in this prison, and at night when we were turned in again, they went to work until nine or ten o'clock; but were then discovered by the guard, who immediately came in and carried two to the Black-hole. In the afternoon, they took two boys at work in the drain before mentioned; and to-day two of those who went out night before last, were brought

back, and another came back of his own accord.

23. Most of this day the prison has been in an uproar, occasioned by a few men that will not be conformable to the rules and articles that we have amongst ourselves, but threaten to take them down and destroy them.

24. This morning we found that our articles were abused, and we took three of the before-mentioned men and tied them up to a post in the prison, and poured cold water down their arms and neck, for the space of half an hour. One of the three was afterwards complained of to the agent, who ordered him to be put in irons, and separated from us.

This afternoon, six more Frenchmen were brought to prison.

25. Yesterday a ship of seventy-four guns, and a frigate, arrived in the Sound, from Admiral Biron's fleet, with two hundred and forty-six sick men on board. The occasion of this ship's coming home was that she had sprung a leak, and the frigate came with her for fear that she might founder at sea.

26. Sunday. I daily expect to hear of an engagement between the English and French fleets, as we have heard several accounts of their being seen in sight of each other.

27. Cool weather for some days past, which is much better for us, as so many of us are confined together.

28. This afternoon we received two letters from Portsmouth prison — one from John Dame, the other from Benjamin Tappan. They give us a very disagreeable account of thirty-nine young men belonging to Newbury, who were lost with Capt. Tracy. Many of their names were mentioned in the latter; some of them I was intimately acquainted with. I could rather wish them in prison with us, than entirely lost.

29. This morning a large three-decker dropped down into the Sound, in order for sailing. Also, we have the London Evening Post, which informs us of the Lively, twenty gun ship, and a frigate, being taken. The last paper before this gives an account of two cutters being taken. They were captured by the French and carried to France.

30. Yesterday was pay-day, and there are a number of men who make it a practice to get drunk every opportunity, and two men last night, who were in liquor, struck and abused two Frenchmen, who were taken in the American service, and the majority of those in prison who were Americans, took their part, and complained to the officer of the guard. The offenders were sent to the Black-hole, and this morning we took the

Frenchmen up stairs with us, where they will not
be abused any more.

31. Yesterday, some in this prison had an invitation by a sentry to go over the wall, but as it was
in the day time, they thought it not proper ; but at
twelve o'clock at night, the same sentry came to
the same place and gave a signal, upon which seven
men went out at a window where one of the iron
bars were loosened, ready to be pulled out. After these seven men got out, the sentry alarmed the
guard, and four of the number were soon taken. If
they had waited a few moments longer, we should
have had a hole in the back side of the prison, for
a number more to have got out. The guard
tell us that they have orders to fire at any one they
see getting over the wall, and also, that the soldier
who let these men go is now under confinement,
and will be either whipped or shot.

This forenoon, Admiral Keppel's fleet arrived
in the Sound. The greatest part of this fleet now
lay where we can see them from this prison. We
hear that they have had an engagement with the
French fleet, but have not learned the particulars.
To-day, also, a dozen more Frenchmen were
brought to prison. Six came out of the Black-
hole ; among whom was Captain Lee. While he
was there, he received a letter from General Burgoyne. There are six remaining there still.

August 1. All that I can say to-day concerning the fleet, is, that several of the ships are very much shattered. Two or three are now lying on their beam-ends, in the Sound, and the boats have been passing and re-passing from them ever since they came in. We have seen a vast number of men come from the ships, in boats, whom we suppose to be wounded, as we are informed that there are between seven and eight hundred wounded men in the royal hospital, who were taken out of the fleet. This is the fleet which they have been raising for the two years past, concerning which they have boasted so much, and which they have called the terror of France. This was England's pride — the fleet that was to sweep the seas, and accomplish such wonders. Alas! many of them are disappointed of their expectations, for in their first engagement they were worsted.

2. A man in prison received a letter from his brother, who is in the fleet. He informed him that he was in the engagement, and there was only twelve sail of the English fleet that engaged the French fleet; but I suppose that he was not allowed to write the particulars.

3. For these two months past, since we have been allowed pens, ink and paper, I have employed them to as much advantage as possible. Most of the time, I have busied myself in writing and cy-

phering. I have had as much writing to do as I
could accomplish; and to-day I sent out to buy
books and instruments to learn navigation. To-
day a number more Frenchmen were brought to
prison.

4. To-day one of the two shattered ships that lay
in the Sound warped up, went to Ammoors, and
the other lays opposite to our prison. To-day I
began to study navigation.

5. A gentleman, who came to see us to-day,
gave in half a guinea, to be drank by the prisoners ; but we thought it better to divide it among
the sick of the respective crews.

6. The masons and carpenters have been at
work repairing an old prison in the yard ; and this
afternoon, as one of the laborers was at work, he
pulled off his coat and hung it up against the prison, in the yard, and left the basket, that he had to
bring slate in, with it. One of the prisoners
went and put on the coat, and put the basket over
his head, and went to the gate ; and the turnkey,
thinking it to be the laborer, let him out. As he
was walking through the street, the laborer met
him, knew his coat, and ran and alarmed the
guard, who went in pursuit of him and soon took
him.

7. We have been waiting impatiently to hear
from the commissioners, for some time past, hoping

that they would settle affairs; but we have had a flying report for some weeks, that they are likely to return as they went, without doing any thing When they first sailed, it was the opinion of many in prison, that they were invested with full power to settle it; but soon after, we were convinced to the contrary.

8. From the Exeter paper we learn that there was only twenty-five sail of the line of battle-ships that engaged the French fleet, and that they had but five hundred and six men killed and wounded; but the royal hospital, where the wounded are, is but a small-arms' shot from this prison, and we have been repeatedly and credibly informed by those who reside in the neighborhood, that there is upwards of a thousand wounded men in the hospital, and a cart is seen to carry away the dead every day. The engagement took place on the 27th of July.

9. Sunday. Last evening, as four men went to empty their tubs, two of them took to the water to swim away, but were soon taken up. The commissioner who was here a few weeks ago, came again to-day, to regulate affairs.

10. This afternoon the guard came in and turned us all out, and locked the doors, which aggravated many, who wanted to be in prison — some reading, some writing, some cyphering, and

some studying navigation. Some went and picked
the locks, opened the doors, and went in ; upon
this the guard came in again, and turned us all
out and placed a sentry at the prison doors.   Two
men, out of spite, went to fighting, and it took most
of the guard to separate them.   Soon after, another fight happened, and about the same time the commissioner came into the yard, and ordered one of
them to be sent to the Black-hole.   In all this disturbance, the officers of the guard appeared very
mild and calm ; they are officers in the militia.
Most of those that have been on guard since we
have been guarded by the militia, have behaved
very well towards us, and very much like gentlemen, as they are chiefly gentlemen of fortune. To-
day the other three men were brought back that
made their escape from prison on the 30th of July,
in the evening.

11. Those who were brought back yesterday,
were sent up out of the Black-hole to-day.   They
tell us that they would not go out again if the
gates were set open ; for they said it is a thing impossible, to get off the island.   While they were
out, they saw a number of ships belonging to Admiral Keppel's fleet, which lay where we cannot
see them from the prison, that were very much
shattered and disabled in the engagement.

12. To-day we were all examined, as of late has

been customary once a month, to see who need clothes, and who do not.

13. Those who wanted shoes, were served to-day. These are allowed by government.

14. This morning, three French prizes were brought into this port — a ship, a brig, and a sloop.

15. This forenoon some officers from the ships, who were sent by Admiral Keppel, came here to take a list of the names of those who have a mind to go on board the men-of-war, and thirty in number gave in their names. Among the number were some Americans, but they were chiefly old countrymen. The officers brought with them an American who was taken with Captain Martingale in the first of the disturbance. His officers gave him a guinea to treat his countrymen.

16. Sunday. To-day another officer came from the ships. He, also, came for men.

17. We hear that Admiral Keppel and his fleet, are to sail in a few days.

18. This afternoon there were five Americans brought to prison. They were all taken in different vessels. Some of them belonged to armed ships, others to merchantmen. Some of them have been taken this six months, and have been hurried about from ship to ship, and used scandalously. They had a bounty offered them to go on

14

board this fleet, now lying in the Sound, but they,
like brave Americans, refused, and chose rather
to come to prison.   They were sent here without
being examined, or committed by any justice of
the peace.

CHAPTER XVI.

AUGUST 19. This afternoon an officer from the ships came for those five men who were brought here yesterday. When they found out that they were to be carried on board the ships, as they were advised by the people in the yard not to go out at the gate, without they were dragged out, like brave men, they resisted, and swore that they would never lift a hand to do any thing on board of King George's ships — neither would they go out of the yard. As the key was turned upon them, the guard was called in, and the officer of the guard and agent plead with them, telling them that they were put in here through mistake; and being over-persuaded by them, they went out.

20. Another French prize was brought in here to-day.

21. It seems that some of the sick and wounded men that came out of Admiral Keppel's fleet, are recovered. They have made several attempts to escape, and they are obliged to keep a guard here to prevent them from running away.

22. Early this morning, part of Admiral Keppel's fleet sailed. Last night, and this morning, a number of Frenchmen were brought to this prison. This afternoon, Captain Lee received a letter from General Burgoyne; he wrote him that he would do all he could to get bail for him.

23. Sunday. Early this morning, the remain der of Admiral Keppel's fleet sailed, except a few ships that are not ready. The squadron that sailed yesterday morning, appeared this morning in sight, off the harbor. I suppose they are all bound on a cruise together.

24. The men that gave in their names, to go on board the men-of-war, are apprehensive that they will not be allowed to do so, and last evening some of them went to work to try to dig out, but upon breaking ground they were discovered, and the sentry discharged two guns into the hole, but they injured no one.

25. To-day, four of the five men who were brought to this prison on the 18th of this month,

and carried away again the next day, were brought back because they would not enter. One of the number was an Italian. He was put in a separate yard, with the Frenchmen. Also, to-day a captain of an armed vessel, that was captured by an American privateer in the North Channel, came here to see Captain Lee. He informed him that he gave bonds, for a large sum of money, to return to America as a prisoner, unless he could get Captain Lee exchanged for him. This man is bound for London.

26. This afternoon a prize was brought in here, which proved to be a large French West Indiaman, a ship of about four hundred tons. Also, a number of French prisoners were brought to prison.

27. We learn from the papers, that the Parliament is prorogued until Thursday the first of October. We also learn from the same source, that the damage to the French fleet, in the late engagement, was very inconsiderable.

28. This morning the guard discovered another hole in the prison, which was begun a few days ago; but as yet there has been but little said about it.

29. We have a paper, from which we learn that Admiral Biron's fleet that sailed from this

port on the 9th of June last, bound to America, upon their passage, met with a gale of wind
which separated the fleet and dismasted several
of their ships.   The Albion has arrived in Lisbon,
dismasted.   She was one of the fleet.

30. Some of us are sick with fever and ague.

31. Some carpenters are now at work building
a new Black-hole, in an old prison in this yard,
that has lately been repaired.

September 1. It is the opinion of some in this
prison, that all the American prisoners in this yard
will be removed to some other prison, to make
room for the French prisoners, as there are now
about four hundred Frenchmen in another yard ;
and there are a great number of French officers
gone into the country, on parole.

2. This afternoon, Mr. Heath and Mr. Sorrey
came to see us, and brought bad news for our officers, in a letter from the committee in London.
The contents read nearly as follows : —

" Not from any prejudice or alteration in our af-
fection for you, but fearing that you will remain
in prison another winter, and the money raised for
your support be expended, we thought proper to
deduct two shillings per week from those officers
who have hitherto been allowed five shillings ; the
other officers and privates, to remain as before."

3. Nothing remarkable.

4. To-day four American gentlemen came to see us; one of whom belonged to Baltimore. He is a young man, and was bound to France to finish his education, when he was taken. He left Amer ica since General Clinton retreated from Philadel phia to New York, and he gave us a very satisfac tory account of the battle — different from what was reported to us before. This young man had liberty to converse with us nearly two hours.

5. This morning, Elias Hart, one of Captain Lee's company, died of consumption in the prison hospital. He is the sixth man that has died since I came to prison. Of late, our sick have fared much better than formerly. As we all draw money once a week, each respective crew contributes, weekly, for their sick, which supplies them with every necessary; so, that of late, there is always some money in the bank for the use of the sick. Since two shillings per week has been deducted from the officers, who formerly received five, most of them, from choice, receive what they are allowed from subscription, in money, and draw no other allowance than what is afforded by government. They can buy provisions as often as they want them, in public market, at the gate.

6. Sunday. This afternoon, three American captains came to see us. They have been taken some months, and are bound directly home. —

Among the number, there is one Captain Potter, belonging to Boston.

7. Several of our men have been taken sick with fever and ague, within a few days, and a great number in prison are unwell.

8. This afternoon, thirteen American prisoners were brought to prison. They were lately brought round from Liverpool, and are the remainder of Captain Ravel's crew.

9. To-day, one Thomas Pillar, of Portsmouth, visited us. He was one of the five who were brought here on the 18th of August; he was carried on board the men-of-war the next day, having been taken in a merchantman. They kept him for a time, but he has since received his discharge, and intends to return home. Several letters were delivered to him to carry, and he is to call and get more.

10. This afternoon, Rev. Mr. Heath came to see us, in company with a young American gentleman, who has been taken, lately, on his passage to France. Our agent, or prison-keeper, being sick and absent, Mr. Heath came into prison and discoursed nearly two hours with the officers.

11. We have accounts in the papers, that Winchester castle is to be repaired for the reception of one hundred American prisoners — a larger number than they now have in England.

12. Captain Burnel, who is a prisoner here, taken in the American service, and has a wife and family in England, has received a letter from his wife, informing him that she has been turned out of doors, wholly on account of his being in the American service. The prisoners are about raising money for her relief.

13. Sunday. This afternoon, Captain Rols received a letter from Captain Harris, in Portsmouth prison. He informs him that forty-five officers and eleven privates, had made their escape lately, out of that prison, twenty-five of whom were brought back — the other thirty-one had got off.

14. We are informed, that last evening, a French privateer was brought in here, with eighty prisoners on board, and the sailors having got a number of prostitutes, and gone below, drinking, the Frenchmen rose, closed the hatches on them, cut the cable and went off with the vessel.

15. To-day, several letters were received here, from the prisoners at Portsmouth. They inform us that they have received a letter from Captain Cowes, in France, who made his escape from that prison. He writes that he has been at Paris, and conversed with Dr. Franklin, and told him our situation. His answer was, that he expected orders from America for the release of all of us. — This agrees with a letter which was received by

15

the prisoners in Portsmouth, from a gentleman in London. In conversation with Mr. Heartley, who is a great speaker in the House of Commons, he informed him, that it lay in Dr. Franklin's power to exchange us when he pleases. It seems by their writing, that they give credit to the report; but our faith has been so long tried, and we have been flattered so often, many in prison will not believe that they are going, until they see the prison gates open.

16. Considerable rain in the first part of the day. I believe there has not been two hours steady rain, before to-day, for nearly three months. To-day some jackets, shirts and stockings were given us by the agent, by order of the Board. I received one shirt, which is the only one I have received from Government, since I have been a prisoner.

17. The West India fleet that put in here a few days ago, sailed to-day, bound up channel. We heard that most of their hands were pressed, and that they were manned by men-of-wars-men. To-day I finished my studies in navigation.

18. To-day Captain Lee received a letter from a man that was here a few weeks ago, and who informed him that he was taken by an American privateer, and came home upon condition that he was to return to America, if he could not get Captain Lee exchanged for him. He now writes that

he has done his utmost, but it is impossible for any man to get out, so long as this Act is in force.

19. To-day about forty French prisoners were brought to prison, who were captured in a privateer. There are now about five hundred French prisoners here.

20. To-day Thomas Pillar came again to see us. He informed us that he expects to sail this afternoon. They are first bound to Ireland, to join a fleet; from thence, to New York. A number in prison sent letters by him. I sent one to my father. He also informs us that he is to work for his passage, and that he has no money to purchase his sea stores. We collected about sixteen shillings, and gave it to him.

21. I expected that Admiral Keppel's fleet would have come in before this time, on account of the sun's crossing the line; but they are not yet in, so that I am in daily expectation of hearing that there has been an engagement between the two fleets.

To-day, eight more of our sick were carried into the prison hospital. They are attacked with fever and ague, and a number more are very unwell with the same complaint; and I am afraid it will be very sickly among us, unless cold weather sets in very soon.

22. To-day is King George's coronation day, and between twelve and one o'clock the fort and garrison fired a salute.   There was but very little firing to what there was last year, on account of there being but few ships in the port.   To-day, also, one Captain Smith came to see us.   He belongs to Portsmouth. He was taken in a merchantman bound to the West Indies, and brought in here.   His men are all put on board the men-of-war; but he has got his liberty, and is bound home.   A great number in prison will send letters by him.'

23. There are a great many in prison, who contemplate having the beef which we receive from subscription, and the soap, tobacco, and oatmeal, and the herbs which we have in our broth, all taken off, and receive a white loaf and some money instead of them.   In order to ascertain the mind of the majority, we all drew up in the yard and passed a vote, which was in favor of the change; but whether the gentlemen, Mr. Heath and Mr. Sorrey, will agree to it or not, we do not know; or whether the agent will allow the money to come into the yard, is not yet determined. I was for receiving the provisions, fearing that if the money was allowed to come into the yard, it would be attended with many bad consequences — too many to enumerate here.

24. This afternoon, Captain Smith came to see us again, and took our letters. I sent one by him to my father. To-day our small beer was very bad, and we refused to take it; they afterwards got some that was a very little better; but a great part in prison carried theirs and turned it over the gate, before the eyes of the prison officers, chosing rather, to drink water. The prison has been in an uproar all day, it being donation day. Several in prison became intoxicated, and went to fighting; but after a few battles the prison was again quiet.

CHAPTER XVII.

SEPTEMBER 25. To-day Captain Ellenwood,
belonging to Beverly, came to see us; he was
taken, but has since been discharged, and is now
bound home. A great number of letters were
sent by him; I sent one to my brother. Last
night, one Captain Rols made his escape from a
separate prison, incognito, and it was not discovered till eleven o'clock to-day; and would not
then have been, had it not been for his messmates,
who, when they drew provisions, told of it; fearing that if they drew for him, they would be
brought into trouble, as there are express orders
against it.

26. To-day two French prizes were brought into this port.

27. Sunday.   Last night, a young man in this prison, having a mind to go on board the men-of-war, made his escape over the wall in a shower of rain, and was not discovered.   He was one of the number that lately petitioned to go on board the ships.   To-day several more of the sick were carried down to the prison hospital. I think there is more than double the number sick now than has been at any time since I have been in prison, except when the small-pox went through the prison. If a man is sick, and very bad, the doctor will take him to the hospital a few days, as a matter of form.   He has served several thus, and sent them up again before they were half recovered, and oftentimes when they were scarcely able to walk.

28. To-day our clothing was examined, as of late has been customary once a month, and as they called the roll they missed the man that made his escape the night before last; but they know when, where, or how he went.

29. We learn, by the paper, that General Carlton has arrived home ; and also that Parliament is prorogued till the 26th of November.

30. Wet, stormy weather, which renders our confinement very tédious.   We are informed that

a few French prisoners, who made their escape a few nights ago, out of a prison in a separate yard, got a boat and set out for France, but meeting with the storm, put about and came back again, and delivered themselves up.

October 1. The first part of last night was very dark, and stormy, and had it not cleared away just as it did before the moon set, immediately after she set there would have been an elopement from this and the officers' prison; but as it was, one Captain Ravel made his escape from the officers' prison, incognito, which I hope hereafter fully to describe. Our new Black-hole is finished to punish Yankees in, and to-day a man was put in for little or nothing — for what they call abusing the turnkey — and ever since he has been in, he has been cutting with a small penknife, and has got a hole through the door near six inches square. To-day nearly one hundred Frenchmen were brought to prison; they were taken in a French East Indiaman.

2. Last night one Mr. Kirk made his escape from the officers' prison; he took the same method that Captains Rols and Ravel did before him.

3. This morning, when the guard came to let the officers out, they missed Captain Ravel and Mr. Kirk, but they knew not when, where, or

how they went, so they made no great stir about them.

4. Sunday. This forenoon a gentleman came with a pardon for thirty-three men that petitioned to go on board the men-of-war, which was nearly as follows :

" His Majesty has been graciously pleased to grant a free pardon to thirty-three men, by name ——-, resident in this prison, upon condition that they will serve, and continue to serve in His Majesty's Navy." This gentleman said that these men are to be taken out of prison to-morrow, but one of the thirty-three has lately made his escape, and we have heard since that he is on board a man-of-war. He also said that those whose names are not on the list, but wish to enter on board the men-of-war, if they would petition, the same course would be taken, and he had no doubt it would be answered to their satisfaction. Accordingly, this, afternoon a petition was written, and about fourteen signed it.

6. Last night there was but very little sleep in this prison, for the men who went on board the men-of-war this morning, were so overjoyed at the thought of being released from prison, that they could not, or would not, sleep the fore part of the night, but ran about the prison, hallooing, and

stamping, and singing, like mad-men, till they were tired out, and then went to bed; but the rest in prison were resolved, as they would not let us sleep the first part of the night, we would not let them sleep the latter; accordingly, we all turned out, and had an Indian Pow-wow, and as solid as the prison is, we made it shake. In this manner we spent the night, and in the morning early the men were called out, twenty of whom were immediately carried on board the Russel ship-of-war, now lying in the Sound. The other twelve were taken out about eleven o'clock, and sent on board the Royal George, now lying in Plymouth dock. As they went out, they gave us three cheers; we returned it, for in joy we parted. Among those who went to-day were about a dozen Americans, but they were chiefly inconsiderate youths. This is a move that I have long wished to see, but it came now very unexpectedly. For my own part, to enter on board a ship of war is the last thing I would do. I would undergo every thing but death before I would think of such a thing. This prison has been a little hell upon earth, but I prefer it as much before a man-of-war, as I would a palace before a dungeon. Ten days ago there were 330 prisoners here, now there are only 294.

6. There is a great alteration to be seen in this prison since those men went away, and I make

no doubt that after another draft, we shall have peace and tranquillity, and live in harmony, and make ourselves happy, considering our situation, to what we have been for months past.

7. This morning, when Mr. Sorrey came to bring us our money, he desired the butcher to tell us that we might depend upon it that a cartel was settled, and that we are very soon to be exchanged for prisoners in France. The strongest circumstance that induces us to believe it is, that those men were admitted on board the men-of-war. This news also agrees with a letter which we received clandestinely from Captain Harris, in Portsmouth prison; he writes that a Rev. gentleman, who has been a friend from the beginning, told him that there was actually a cartel negotiating.

8. Nothing remarkable, but repeated confirmations of what we have heard before.

9. It is four months to-day since Admiral Biron's fleet sailed from the Sound, and as yet we have heard of no arrival, except one ship. Also, this afternoon the brewer that supplies us with beer, through a mistake brought a cask of strong beer instead of malt, and he did not find out his mistake until he got here, and so was obliged to carry it back again. Afterwards, he brought us some that was small enough, and was not according to contract; we received it, but several took

15*

theirs and turned it over the gate. The man that was put in the Black-hole, nine days ago, has ever since been punished unjustly, and to-day he was resolved to get out, and we were resolved to get him out. After tearing the Black-hole yard down, which is about twenty feet long and eight wide, he got out and came into this prison, and in the afternoon the whole guard came in with their arms, and demanded the man. But, with one accord, we all said that he should not be punished unjustly, and if they put him in the Black-hole it should not stand an hour. All this time the man had posted himself advantageously upon a beam over head in this prison, with a large stone in each hand, and a stocking full besides, swearing, in a most determined manner, that he would crack the first man's skull that offered to touch him. The guard went in to persuade him to go peaceably, but he would not, and they dared not, or did not touch him; and after a long controversy, they went out without him.

10. We learn, by the papers, that the Fox frigate, and a ship of eighteen guns, and one of sixteen guns, are taken by the French and carried into France.

11. Sunday. To-day we received a pound of potatoes per man, instead of cabbage, which the late draught has rendered very scarce.

12. To-day three letters were received in this prison, from prisoners in Portsmouth. They agree concerning the cartel which is expected to take place. They write that passports are signed and passed from Dr. Franklin to the ministry. They write, also, that they had it from the American agent in Paris.

13. To-day, a fleet consisting of fifty sail, with convoy, passed this harbor. We suppose them to be an outward bound West India fleet.

14. Last night Captain Lee made his escape from the officers' prison, in the same manner that Captain Rols and others did, before him; and there are several others who are fixed, and only waiting for an opportunity to go the same way.

15. It is twenty-three months to-day since I left Newbury. This morning when the guard counted the officers out, they missed one; and after a long search, they found it to be Captain Lee. But all they know about it, is that he is gone.

16. As it is twelve months to-day since General Burgoyne was taken, in commemoration thereof, at one o'clock, we all drew up in the yard, and gave three cheers; and at night, before we were turned in, we did the same. This afternoon, seven more American prisoners were brought to prison. They were lately brought from Liverpool, and were captured in different vessels.

17. For two days past, there have been no doctors here to attend to our sick, and I hear that the chief physician at the royal hospital has the charge of them. To-day a number were removed into this prison, from a separate prison, called the itchy ward, to make room for the sick. The masons are now at work, building a chimney in an old prison, in this yard, that has lately been repaired. This prison is to be made an hospital for the sick, as the other hospital is wanted for the French prisoners; for there is between five and six hundred of them in one large prison, in a separate yard, and they are very sickly. They have the spotted fever among them, which was brought by those taken in the French East Indiaman.

18. Sunday. Yesterday the officers in the other prisons received a private letter from without, which confirms the news concering a cartel, giving the particulars, which causes great satisfaction in the yard.

19. A man in prison received a letter from the Russell, ship-of-war, which is now lying in the Sound, from those who went on board from this prison. They write that they are bound to a station in the East Indies.

20. This morning a pardon arrived from the King, for the fourteen men who petitioned to go on board the King's ships.

21. This morning, the same man that brought the first draft, came, and called over the names of those fourteen men, and asked them of what country they were, and how long they had been to sea. Two of them being sick of their bargain, denied that their names were there.

I am in hopes of soon hearing that Rhode Island is taken, for I hear that the British troops there, have burnt five frigates and two sloops-of-war, fearing that they would fall into the hands of the Americans. From the same source we learn that the Albion, a ship of sixty-four guns, is taken by the French, and carried into France. — Also, that four sail of the line have lately sailed form France, bound to America, to join Count D' Estaing; and also, that the English have taken another East Indiaman from the French, besides that which was brought in here.

22. To-day some officers from the ships came after those men, and the two before mentioned denied that they signed their names. They did not ask them to go, but one man went that did not sign, so that on the whole they got thirteen, which, with the first draft, makes forty-five men that have gone on board the men-of-war. But those who remain, I believe, are true sons of America.

23. Notwithstanding the encouragement we have about being exchanged, last evening a man

made his escape by getting over the wall. It being very dark and rainy, more would have gone the same way, but they were discovered by the guard.

24. It is twenty-two months to-day, that I have been a prisoner; but now I think the auspicious day is at hand, when, with God's blessing, we shall all take our departure from this place. If I mistake not, this is the only day since I have been a prisoner, that we have not been counted. But this morning we were let out, and at night turned in, without any such thing; so that it appears they grow very careless about us to what they have been, which I consider a good omen.

25. Sunday. One hundred and one Sundays have passed since I have enjoyed a Sabbath day's privilege. To-day being King Charles' restoration day, the garrison and fort fired a salute.

CHAPTER XVIII.

Oil of tar for Prison — Frenchmen break out -- One Shot — Reduction of
Donation — Two Americans in Irons — Various opinions about the Cartel — Several Holes in hand-- Fearful Apprehensions -- Dominica taken
by the French and Americans — King's Troops on Martha's Vineyard
— Drunken Prisoners delivered up — Forbearance of the Guard — Fire
in the Black-hole — Four American Boys — Dolton as Fortune Privateer — Base Treachery — Plans Discovered — Mitchell the Villain
— Letter of Thanks — Two Years from Home — Unsuccessful Attempts.

OCTOBER 26. It is twenty-three months to-day,
since we sailed in the brig Dolton from Portsmouth. It is a long time since this prison was
smoked, so that it is exceedingly foul, and smells
very offensive. To-day, by order of Dr. Far, the
principal physician of the royal hospital, who has
now the care of our sick, some stuff was procured,
which they tell us is the oil of tar, which was put
on the posts fore and aft the prison, above and below. They inform us that it is better than smoking.
Be it as it may, it gives the prison a very disagreeable smell.

27. As the evenings are now of considerable length, although we are not allowed candles, yet we have them every night, and have had them for several weeks past.

28. Last night the French prisoners broke out of their prison, through a hole which they had dug several yards under ground. I cannot learn the exact number that got out. However, they were discovered by the guard and pursued, and one of them was shot through the breast. After which, a turnkey struck him on the head with an iron poker, but he is yet alive. The Frenchmen are very sickly ; they have the spotted fever amongst them, which carries off great numbers.

This morning, Mr. Heath and Mr. Sorrey came to see us, and informed us that they had received a letter from the committee, in London, with orders to deduct sixpence per week from each officer, and ninepence from each private ; so that for the future, the officers are to receive two shillings and sixpence each, per week, and privates one shilling and threepence each, per week. All the reason I can assign for this change, is, that the donation grows short.

29. The camp at Coxheath is now broken up, and the Somersetshire militia, with the 13th regiment, have removed to the barracks at Plymouth dock ; so that one day we are guarded by

the militia, and the other by the 13th regiment.—
To-day, about fifty Frenchmen were removed from
a separate prison, in another yard, to the prison-
ship, for want of room in that prison.

30. To-day Mr. Sorrey came and answered a
petition which we sent out, to receive what we are
allowed in money, as it is so trifling. Mr. Sorrey
says that Mr. Heath is absent, so that he will continue the provisions until he returns, and then he
will consult him.

31. We learn, from the papers, that Lord Howe
and Sir George Johnston, have arrived home in
the Eagle man-of-war, of sixty-four guns.

November 1. This afternoon two Americans
were brought to the gate, in irons, having four or
five men, with pistols, guarding them; but who
they were, or where they were taken, I cannot tell.
I suppose, however, that they were not committed, by their being carried away again.

2. It is almost four weeks since Mr. Sorrey told
us that we were to be exchanged; and some in
prison, who believed it at first, begin to think it
very doubtful; some did not believe it at first. For
my own part, I am persuaded it is true, and believe it will be soon — how soon I cannot tell; but
every day since I heard of it, seems as long as a
week before.

3. At this time we have several holes in hand,

one of which was discovered this morning, by some
dirt that was carried out in the tubs to the edge
of the river, to empty.   To-day two large two-
deckers came in, which, I suppose, belong to Admiral Keppel's fleet ; and hear that they are all in
Portsmouth, and other ports.   I also hear that the
Ocean, a three-decker, a ship of ninety guns,
which came in a few days ago in a storm which
she experienced, sprung a leak, and threw overboard most of her guns.

4. To-day Mr. Sorrey came, and brought some
money for the officers, but none for us, as our
provisions for the week past amounts to what we
are allowed.   Mr. Sorrey says that he expects the
cartel very soon.   The Lord have mercy upon us,
if it does not arrive before the donation is all expended, for the second death will be worse than
the first.

5. To-day, being gunpowder treason, at one
o'clock the garrison and fort fired a salute, and the
bells in Plymouth have been chiming most of the
day.

6. To-day about one hundred more of the
French prisoners in another yard, were removed
on board the Cambridge, a prison ship.   For several days past, a number of men have been at work
laying the foundation of a large prison hospital,
which is to be built.

It has been strongly reported this week, that Dominica has been taken by the French and Americans, and this evening I had the pleasure of seeing it confirmed, in the paper, by authority. The Lieutenant Governor of that Island is now a prisoner in France.

7. We learn, by the paper, that the King's troops in America, have been to Martha's Vineyard, disarmed the inhabitants, and demanded ten thousand sheep and five hundred oxen.

8. Sunday. Nothing very remarkable. Various conjectures concerning a cartel. Some imagine it is to come from France; others think it will be fitted out in England, and others are doubtful if it will come at all.

9. I thought that all who had any idea of going on board the men-of-war, had gone; but I understand that a number have sent their names out, to go; how many I cannot tell, as they did it very slyly. We shall know who they are, and how many, when an order comes to take them out.

10. This morning two of our men got some liquor, clandestinely, and made themselves drunk. One of these, about twelve o'clock, went to the gate to buy some strong beer, which was denied him, and being in a passion, without any provocation, he swore that he would break the agent's windows, and took up some old shoes, bones and

stones, and threw them till he had broken seven squares in one window, and one in another, in the front of the agent's office. There being three of them intoxicated, one of them took hold of the sentry at the gate, and would have taken his gun from him, but the guard came in, and the captain of the guard took hold of one of them, and being a militia man, and a very great gentleman, he said that he was lothe to bring his men who were armed, against us who were unarmed, and so went out. Upon which, we took one of them ourselves and pitched him out of the gate by the nape of the neck, and so delivered him up. In the afternoon, after we were turned out, we took the other two and delivered them up. All of which were sent to 'the Black-hole. So, that if any man misbehaves and deserves punishment, we will deliver him up, or punish him ourselves, rather than he should go unpunished; but rather than see a man chastised unjustly, we will do our utmost for his rescue. As for instance, on the 19th of October, when we released one of these same men from the Black-hole.

11. Those three men who were put in the Black-hole yesterday, employed themselves last night, in cutting through the bulkhead that separates the Black-hole from the hospital, and piled up the chips and set them on fire. Where they

obtained the fire we cannot tell, but they were soon glad enough to put it out, as the smoke increased. This afternoon four American boys came to see us, that were taken with Captain Claston, in the Freedom, above twelve months ago. Those boys were detained, and now belong to the Apollo frigate.

12. As a fortnight has passed, and we have received no money, we begin to fear that we shall receive no more; but what is left of the donation, I expect we shall receive in clothes and provision; and for that reason, and the want of employment, I to-day began to make boxes.

13. We learn, from the paper, that the Fortune privateer, Captain George Tarton, which was formerly the Dolton, has made more money by privateering, than any other privateer out of England, since the commencement of hostilities between the English and French.

14. Last evening, it being dark and rainy, two holes were opened at the back part of the prison, and five men went out. They had agreed with a soldier to let them pass for so much money. This soldier's name was Mitchell; he was once a stage-driver in America. He let them out, and they gave him two pounds nineteen shillings; but after they delivered him the money, he let them out where the guard stood ready to receive them and

carry them to the Black-hole.   This morning, the
guard went into the officers' prison and discovered
a hole under the stairs, where they had dug down
about six feet, and then proceeded through the
guard-house and came up under the guard bed. —
They then went up stairs and demanded the keys
of the officers' chests, which they opened, and
found a suit of uniform which one of the officers
had purchased to make his escape in.   This was
the method Captains Rols, Ravel, Lee, and Mr.
Kirk took to make their escape, — following the
guard out when they used to come at night; but
this scheme is blasted.   The hole in the officers'
prison had been finished near a month, and they
had been only waiting for an opportunity to put
their plans into execution; but as this Mitchell
has appeared to be a friend, I suppose that some
one of the officers communicated it to him, and he
informed his officer; so by that means it was discovered.

This afternoon Mr. Sorrey and Mr. Heath came
to see us, and we presented them with a letter of
thanks for the many favors we have received at
their hands, and requested them to let us have
part of what we are to receive, in money.   This
favor we probably shall obtain.   We have not received any coals from government, for the comfort
of our sick in the hospital, for nearly six weeks,

but have been obliged to use the donation coals. We informed Mr. Heath and Mr. Sorrey of this, and we find that we have been cheated, by the agent and doctor, out of nearly forty bushels of coals.

15. Sunday. It is two years to-day since I left Newbury. Alas! little did I think that I should be here now. Last night, a hole that we have had in hand nearly a fortnight, unfortunately foundered in the street. This hole was dug down by the side of the prison, about ten feet, and our intention was to dig across the street under ground, into a garden on the opposite side of the way; but, by the time it was half across, it foundered.

16. Night before last, we heard a firing which we could not account for. We have since heard that the Royal George ran ashore from her moorings, but was got of again with but little trouble.

CHAPTER XIX.

NOVEMBER 17. Tuesday. I am twenty-one
years of age. Alas! little did I think, three years
ago, that at this age I should have spent so much
of my time immersed in prison. A sorrowful
freedom this; or rather no freedom at all. There
has been nothing to be purchased within these
walls to-day, to drink, but cold water, and we
came near having nothing to eat; for, it being
rainy last night, some in prison broke a hole
through the wall, with the intent to go out, but
were discovered, and this morning our butcher

went out to cut the meat up, but the agent put all
in prison on half allowance, and then went off.
When the butcher came in, we told the cooks not
to cut the meat up, for we would not receive half
allowance. About 4 o'clock in the afternoon the
agent came back, in a great passion, swearing by
all that was good or bad, that all in this prison
should go on half allowance. The men that dug
the hole offered to go to the Black-hole, but he
refused their offer; but after a long controversy,
he became a little more calm, and took the men
and gave us our allowance, which we received
about dark.

18. For several days past, a large number of
men have been at work upon an island, called
Drake's Island. It seems that they have been
building new works; I suppose for fear that a land-
ing may be attempted by the French; and another
fort is building further up the river.

19. To-day Joseph Burnham, one of our company, who had his leg cut off some months ago,
has so far recovered as to come up into this yard.

20. We learn, by the papers, that 10,000 troops
are to be sent to America in the spring, and the
war is to be pushed with the utmost vigor, both by
sea and land.

21. To-day we received a letter from Mr. Sorrey and Mr. Heath, which informs us that the beef

shall be deducted, which we have received by subscription, and the other articles continued as before, and that we shall receive sixpence per week
in money, according to our request.

22. Sunday. Wet, dirty weather, as it has
been for three or four weeks past, in which time
there has scarcely been a day in which it has not
rained more or less.

23. This evening I had the privilege of hearing
the London Evening Post read, which is a paper
we seldom see, and in which is a burlesque on the
Ministry, very severe.

24. I have been a prisoner three-and-twenty
months to-day.

25. To day we received sixpence per man, and
the beef was deducted; the rest of the provisions
continue, which, with sixpence per week, amounts
to what we are allowed — fifteen pence, as before
mentioned. This afternoon, the men in the Black-
hole, being vexed by ill usage, and not being allowed to come out and take the air, broke down the
Black-hole door, which alarmed the guard, and
the agent ordered five of them to be put in irons;
but the militia being on guard, and the officer being a great gentleman, he put only one of them in
irons.

26. It is two years to-day since we sailed in the

brig Dolton from Portsmouth. To-day the Parliament is to set, according to adjournment.

27. Wet, rainy, blustering, unsteady weather, which renders our confinement more tedious than in good weather, on account of our being obliged to keep house a great part of the time. At present, many in prison are destitute of shoes, and of late our prison has become very leaky. Along through the last of summer and the first of fall, for nearly three months, there was scarcely rain enough to wet the dust; but now, for a month past, there has been scarcely a day but there has been more or less rain; so that the grass in the fields looks much better now than it did in the month of August, when the fields were parched up for want of rain.

28. Nothing remarkable.

29. Sunday. To-day William Moody came to see us; I had not the least expectation of ever seeing him again in these parts, for I expected that he had got home before this, as he was cleared a long time ago. Where he has been ever since I cannot tell, but he tells us that he is now a carpenter of a privateer of eight guns, belonging to this port, in which he has been one cruise, and taken one French St. Domingo vessel.

30. Nothing remarkable.

December 1. This evening I had the privilege

of reading the London Evening Post, in which is
an account of the capture of three English frigates, by name the Minerva and the Acton, carried into the West Indies, and the Thundering
Unicorn, into Boston.

2. This afternoon, one John Howe came to see
us. He made his escape out of this prison
a few months ago, and went on board the Blenheim, a guard ship in this port; and as he was
one that petitioned to go on board the men-of-
war, after he made his escape his pardon came
down for him with the test; so that he may come
on shore, as often as he can get liberty, with safety. He induced two of the number who petitioned last to run away, at night, when they went out
with their tubs, which they did, and a boy with
them, but they were pursued by the guard, taken,
and lodged in the Black-hole.

3. The three that were put in the Black-hole
last night were taken out to-day. To-day I had
the opportunity of seeing and reading the King's
speech on the 26th of last month, in which he
seems very cool and moderate to what he was at
the opening of the session last year. His speech
was not long, but too long to be comprehended
here; but he confesses that his arms have not met
with the success that the justness of the cause and
their exertions promised; and I think that he

seems rather inclined to peace, as he says, if it can be attained consistently with the honor and dignity of the crown.

4. This evening we had two papers in prison, the Exeter paper and the London Evening Post; in the latter were the proceedings of Parliament. This paper says that the King was never seen to look so melancholy, and to speak so sorrowful, as on the 26th of Nov. last; and he was never seen to exert himself, except when he addressed the House of Commons for support. In the same paper are several fine speeches in favor of America; they lament the loss of Dominica, and deplore the situation of Great Britain and all her foreign territories.

5. Last evening Mr. Anthony Shomaker privately made his escape from the officers' prison, and but very few in this yard knew any thing of it until this evening; and neither the agent nor the guard know it yet, which makes it well for the mess he left, as they draw his provisions. But this is not the only thing; the reason we keep it from them is that he may have a better chance to get off, and to screen the militia on guard at the time.

6. Sunday. By this time I begin to feel very sad about our cartel, for I expected that it would have been here before this time, but I en-'ertain the same opinion, about its being agreed

upon, now, as I did at first; I am fearful, however, that something has turned up to prevent its being put in execution.

7. We were all called to muster just before night. We thought it was on account of Mr. Shomaker being gone, but we were soon convinced to the contrary, as they did not find it out till his name was called; and I have heard since that the Board sent down for an immediate list of all the prisoners here. There are various conjectures concerning this uncommon affair; some are encouraged by it, others not.

8. We learn, from the papers, that there are 7000 English prisoners in and about Brest.

9. To-day Mr. Coudry, the agent, and Mr. Turner, his clerk, told us that we should be exchanged very soon; it was but a few days ago that they contradicted the story concerning a cartel, and wanted to entice us to enter on board the men-of-war, so that I pay no regard to what they say, whether it be for us, or against us.

10. To-day the story concerning a cartel is rumored again; we are told that the transports are engaged for that purpose; and some say that we shall be gone in a fortnight, others in a month.

11. At this time, there is considerable bad money in prison, which was brought and handed in as change for good money, by some of the turn-

keys or market people, and now that they begin
to be suspicious of our going away soon, they will
take no more of it, though it has passed in and
out for several months, so that there is considerable laying on our hands, which we are obliged
to lose. Some in prison have several shillings in
bad half pence.

12. I fear that I shall forever have cause to remember this day, to my sorrow ; for this morning,
when we were turned out, it was reported from
the officers' prison that the Act by which we were
committed was again renewed, but upon further
inquiry, and upon searching the paper, we found
it to be nearly as follows : Sir Gray Cooper made
a motion in the House for leave to bring in a bill
to renew this act, for a certain limited time, which
passed without a debate. But the worst is yet to
come; Mr. Heath and Mr. Sorrey, who hitherto
have been messengers of good news, came this
afternoon with tidings of bad news, in a letter
from the committee in London, which gives an account of all the donation being expended. This
occasions many long faces in prison ; but in this
letter there is a word of comfort, for they write
that the time is so short which we have to stay in
prison, that they thought it not worth while to
open a new subscription, though they have the
same feelings for us that they ever had ; which

seems to imply, that if it was necessary, or if we were to stay here long, they would do it again.

13. Sunday. The sudden, disagreeable, and unexpected news that we received yesterday, has greatly added to our affliction, and this is the last day that we may expect any thing from the donation. To-day we received a fourpenny white loaf per mess, which came last night; so that from this time we may bid it adieu. This donation has lasted exactly eleven months and one day; so that it was eleven months yesterday since we received the first of it. Doubtless many of us would have been in our graves before this day, had it not been for this; and heaven, I hope, will reward the donors.

14. To-day we received another fourpenny loaf per mess; the occasion of it I cannot tell. Last evening, about eight o'clock, Mr. Hyfield made his escape from the officers' prison, in disguise; and about ten o'clock another attempted it in the same way, but was discovered, and sent to the Black-hole. There are a number sick in another prison in this yard, which is called a hospital; but it is not worth the name, as there is no fire-place in it, neither is it water tight, but whenever it rains, as it has done most of the time of late, it beats in upon the sick as they lay in their beds. At this time there are several sick with the fever,

three of whom now appear to be at the point of death.

15. Last evening John Lott died with fever; he was an Indian that was taken with Captain Brown, in the sloop Charming Sally. He is the seventh man that has died in prison since I came here, and he is the seventh that Captain Brown has lost of his men since he was taken. Six of our crew have died since we were taken, two of Captain Lee's, and one of Captain Henry Johnson's. There are two men in prison who lay dangerously sick, and to-day we got leave for Mr. Heath to come and pray with them, which is the only public prayer that has been made in this yard since we came to prison. I think it not amiss to mention a few words that this Rev. gentleman said concerning the sick. He said that they should be supplied with such necessaries as they wanted for their comfort, if he had to go about the country with a bag and beg them. To-day we came upon our old government allowance, which, I must confess, is better than it was in 1777; the quantity is the same, except half a pint of peas on Saturday, which we were then cheated out of; our beef and bread are the same in quantity, but better in quality. To-day the agent served out a few clothes to such as were in immediate need, but poor Charles gets none.

16. To-day the sick were removed from one prison, in this yard, to another that has been some time preparing for them. ˉ

17. Yesterday the captain of the grenadiers in the 13th regiment was on guard; last evening he came into this prison and used two or three men very ill. As this man has lately boasted that no man could make his escape while he was on guard, and as they had not found out that Mr. Hyfield was gone, who made his escape several evenings ago, and on account of the captain's insolence and abuse last evening, we let them know it this morning, so that they think he went away on this captain's guard, and the blame, if there is any, will fall upon his head. To-day, by the request of the whole prison, a letter of thanks was written, and sent to the honorable committee in London, and we desired that it might be made public, by putting it in the paper. As there was something in it which we did not wish the agent to see, we sent it out by the officer of the guard, who, being a gentleman in the militia, and approving mightily of it, promised to forward it on its way.

18. A report has prevailed in prison, to-day, that information has been received that two ships have been engaged, in Portsmouth, to carry us to Boston.

19. Last night Captain Alexander Ross made his escape from the officers' prison. Our officers that have made their escape so many times lately, may thank good friends and their money for getting off; but a poor foremast hand, with no friends, and no money in his pocket, would stand but a poor chance to get off, if he was without the walls.

CHAPTER XX.

DECEMBER 20. We learn, by the papers, that the ministry are resolved to carry on another campaign in America ; and, if they can do nothing else, spread horror and depredation from one end of the continent to the other. They have a new mode for carrying on the war ; as I believe they have given up all idea of conquering the country. They mean now, to destroy their seaports, and render the country of as little use to France as possible ; but poor old England is in a deplorable situation, and this, I believe, will be her last dying struggle.

THE SURPRISE. p 206.

Thirty-one lords have drawn up a protest against this new system of war, to warn the public and to screen themselves from the evil that may fall upon those who persist in this inhuman and bloody conflict.

21. There has been no answer to the last petition that was sent to the Board; and to-day another petition was written and signed by a considerable number. This short allowance strikes such a dread upon a great number in this prison, that I am afraid it will frighten many, and induce them to go on board the men-of-war, who otherwise would have no thoughts of going. For my own part, I have received about a half a guinea for boxes, of late, but if I had not a farthing it would be equally the same, for as long as I can get provision enough to keep body and soul together, I shall prefer this prison to a man-of-war.

22. Last evening Mr. Salter made his escape from the officers' prison. Captain Boardman attempted it, but was discovered, and put in the Black-hole.

We learn, by the papers, that the high treason Act is again renewed; for how long a time, is uncertain.

23. To-day Mr. Heath came and served out the remainder of the clothes, that were left of the donation. I received only a pair of shoes. This is

the last that we may expect from the donation, either in provisions or clothes, though we are allowed oatmeal to thicken our broth, and coals to burn; which are given, as I suppose, by private gentlemen.

24. It is two years to-day since we were taken. To-day a paper was drawn up in prison, to discover who and how many were of a side, and to hasten those who have a desire to petition, and to prevent petitioning hereafter; for we have reason to think it has already been of great damage to us. The contents of the paper were as follows :

" We, whose names are hereunto subscribed, do, of our own free and voluntary consent, agree firmly with each other, and hereby solemnly swear, that we are fully determined to stand, and so remain as long as we live, true and loyal to our Congress, our country, our wives, children and friends, and never to petition to enter on board any of His Britannic Majesty's ships or vessels, or into any of his services whatsoever."

The above was signed by upwards of a hundred. I was one of the number. Some of the number that did not sign this, would not go on board of a man-of-war any sooner than those that did sign it.

25. This is Christmas, and a sorrowful one it is, though we had sent us, by our friends without,

a fourpenny white loaf per mess, and a little cabbage. Little did I think, last Christmas, of being here now; neither did I expect, three months ago, to be here to-day. But all signs seem to fail; and it seems as though we were enchanted here. A third year of our imprisonment has begun.

26. We learn, by the papers, that Admiral Keppel is to receive a trial by court martial, for his behavior on the 27th of July last, in an engagement with the French fleet, off Brest. He is confined to his house, with two sentrics at his door.

27. Sunday. At this time, we have a hole in hand, which we began near a month ago. This hole is dug down by the side of the prison, about nine feet perpendicular, and from thence it is dug about fifteen feet under ground, across a road; and our intention is to dig up into a garden on the other side of the way. A great quantity of dirt has already come out of this hole, and we have much trouble in concealing it. We have filled every hole and corner in the prison where we can with safety hide it, and a great many large stones are laid fore and aft the prison, in piles, under our hammocks, with old garments laid over them. — There has been so many holes discovered of late, in this prison, that we are very cautious how we proceed with this. We work only when the mili-

18

tia are on guard, which is every other day, because
they are not so suspicious and exact in searching,
as the 13th regiment.

28. We have now got the hole almost completed, and mean to put our plan into execution
to-night, and I hope God will be with us.   Never
did I know the true value of money until now; if
I had four or five guineas, I could scarcely have a
doubt of my liberty ; but from the want of this I
expect to be brought back again if I should have
the good fortune to get out.   While I now write,
we are dividing ourselves into companies, to cast
lots who shall go out first, so as to give every one
an equal chance that intends to go ; except three
that dug the hole — they are to go first.   I believe
that nearly one half in prison intend to go, if possible ; but I fear that but very few will get out
before we shall be discovered, on account of their
being four walls to get over, about eight feet high,
each, after we get into the garden, and before we
get into the road.

29. Last night we opened the hole and shut it
up again, until about twelve o'clock.   We then
opened it again, and a man went out and opened
a window in the first wall.   We likewise chose
two of the principal men in prison, that did not intend to go, to take the list of each company, and
stand one upon each side the hole, to see that ev-

ery man went out in his turn.   It fell to my lot to
go out in the first company, after those who dug
the hole.   I went through, and came to the first
wall, where the window was open.   Three more
walls I had to get over, which were so high that I
could just jump and catch the tops of them; all of
which, we went over like greyhounds.   Then six
of us met and concluded to go together.   We then
ran back into the country until we judged we were
two or three miles out of Plymouth, and in this
manner we rambled about the fields, up hill and
down dale, over hedges and through ditches, till
we were lost and could not find the right road to
Tinemouth, which was the town we meant to aim
for, about thirty-six miles from Plymouth.   Before
we were lost, we walked about twenty miles, as
we judged, backwards and forwards, through the
fields.   We then sat down by the side of a hill, till
we were almost chilled to death.   We then proceeded to a haystack, under the lee of which we lay
until the day began to break, and it being cloudy,
we could not discover the east from the west; so
we wandered about till daylight, when we found
the road to Tinemouth, and pressed forward till
we came to a bridge, where, by the help of a mile-
stone, we found, to our great surprise, that we
were only three miles from Plymouth.   At this
bridge I pulled of a pair off trowsers, which I wore

to keep my breeches and stockings clean, and threw them into the stream. We then pushed on two miles farther, in the road. By this time, the people began to stir about, and we concluded it was no longer safe to walk by daylight. We then took a cross road that led into the country, and travelled about a mile, and then cut across some fields, and went into a hedge, where we determined to lay till night, and then proceed on our journey. It was almost seven o'clock in the morning when we went into the hedge, and we lay there undiscovered, as we supposed, until an hour before sunset. All this time, we lay on the wet grass, and had nothing to eat or drink. We had only a penny loaf apiece, and that we meant to save to eat in the night following, and so travel all night; the next morning we expected to reach Tinemouth. About nine hours we lay in the hedge, wet, hungry, and almost chilled to death with the cold; lying all the time in one position, longing for the night to come. I went to stir one of my legs and a bone snapped and went out of joint, and as one of the company was setting it, about ten farmers, with a soldier, came upon us. One of them had a pistol, one a bayonet, one a flail, and all the rest had clubs; we told them that we came into Plymouth in a prize, and were bound to Tinemouth. The country was

alarmed, and we were taken.   They carried us to
a little village and gave us a good glass of brandy,
and a half penny cake, apiece.   We were then
guarded by a sergeant of the militia, and about a
dozen farmers, to Plymouth.   We stopped on the
road to get something to drink, but they would not
let us stop to eat.   We came to Plymouth in the
evening, and some hundred men gathered round
us and caused great confusion and excited a tu-
multuous broil.   In this fray I lost my penny loaf.
From thence we were brought to prison again,
where we found that about thirty were taken
before us, and the Black-hole was full ; so that we
were put in the long prison again.   I was here informed that one hundred and nine men got out at
this hole, and that it was carried on with the greatest regularity, till a boy went out who was unable
to get over the wall, and he called for help, which
alarmed the guard ; otherwise, every man in prison
might have got out, that had any inclination to do
so.

30. Last night and to-day, about forty more were
brought back, and those in the Black-hole taken
out, and all put on half allowance.

31. To-day a number more were brought back,
and those of us who are on short allowance, are
divided into messes, eight men in a mess, all to sit
down to a four pound loaf, and three pounds of
beef, before it is cooked, a bowl of broth, and a

little cabbage, which we have only every other day. To-day a mess of us joined together and bought a bag of potatoes, of fifteen gallons, for two shillings and ninepence, which will be of great service to us, on our forty days' half allowance.

January 1, 1779. This is a new year, and a sorrowful one it is, though our friends sent us a white loaf to every mess on full allowance, and would have sent one to those on half allowance, but our cruel agent would not let it come in. This so vexed us that me went and reasoned the case with him, and he at last consented to let it come in, if it was intended only as a new year's gift. We have also received greens, for four days past, instead of cabbage or peas, which is not half so good as either. We have to-day written a petition to the Board to see if they will grant us peas, and another, to see if they will favor us in regard to provision or time, while on half allowance. Two more men were brought back this afternoon. As yet, I have not got over my frolic. My knee is stiff where I put it out of joint. My hands are sore, being torn with burs. In short, I have not got a place about me the size of a halfpenny, but what is stiff and sore.

2. To-day we wrote a note to Mr. Heath, to let him know that Mr. Coudry had consented to let a loaf come in to each mess on half allowance, as a new year's gift. Also, to-day the agent served out

shoes to almost every man in prison, except those on half allowance. We have received a letter from Portsmouth, which informs us that fifteen men had gone from that prison on board the men-of-war, last week, and that there are two hundred and thirty American prisoners there.

3. Sunday. In answer to the note we sent yesterday, to Mr. Heath, we received a white loaf to each mess on half allowance, and the generosity of our friends led them to send us a sixpenny loaf, which make our hearts glad.

4. Notwithstanding there are so many of us on half allowance, it does not discourage us from digging, for yesterday we began another hole, and last night it was unfortunately discovered.

This afternoon another man was brought back, who had got as far as Torbay, where he saw three hundred sail of vessels, in three fleets, one of which was bound to New York, one to Halifax, and the other to the West Indies, most of them with provisions, and some troops.

5. Last night, Captain Boardman made his escape from the officers' prison, and as there has been none brought back to-day, it gives us reason to hope, that those who are now out, will escape from this detested place. The number not yet returned is twenty-four, as eighty-five out of one hundred and nine have been brought back again.

6. This morning, I began to set myself up to sell bread, to enlarge the little amount of money I have, while on half allowance. I send out to the baker's and purchase by the dozen, and retail it out; by which means I realize twopence on a dozen. As necessity is the mother of invention, so necessity obliges me to take every honest method to get a penny, especially at this time, when we have greens, or cabbage as they are called, instead of peas, but unworthy of the name of either, for it is more like kelp than cabbage, and it is not fit for any human being to eat.

7. To-day a gentleman came to the gate and gave in a crown, to be divided among ninety of us in prison, who are on half allowance. This crown gains a reprieve for a dog, which keeps in the yard and belongs to some of the officers on guard. This dog we are resolved to kill and eat, in a few days, as necessity will oblige us to do so. This evening two more men were brought back, who went out on the 28th of December. They were taken about forty miles distant, at a place called Exmouth. There are now only twenty-two out, as eighty-seven have been brought back. We are told that five pounds a head is given for every one that is taken up; if so, it has cost government four hundred and thirty-five pounds for the eighty-seven that are brought back.

CHAPTER XXI.

JANUARY 8. It is two years, to-day, since we arrived in this Sound. One of those that were brought back yesterday, brought a paper in with him, in which is an account of an hurricane that happened about ten days ago, at London, in which a great number of houses were blown down; and by the same tornado, a great many vessels were cast away, at Margate Roads, and a number of lives lost. Among the rest was an East Indiaman. By the paper, we also learn, that a great part of Greenwich Hospital was consumed by a fire that took place there.

19

This is a much worse time to be on short allowance than any time since we have been in prison.
As there are so many on half allowance, those who
are on full allowance, and are willing to help us,
are unable, for their own allowance is not sufficient
to support nature ; and the half of that is intolera-
ble. There are numbers in prison on half allowance who have not a penny to help themselves
with. New shoes have been sold for a shilling,
and new shirts for the same price, by persons who,
perhaps, had no others to wear ; in short, there are
a great many long faces in prison, for nothing but
hunger rages throughout. To such a degree is
this the case, that we killed a dog this afternoon,
in order to let him cool by to-morrow, and his in-
sides were scarcely out, before his liver was on
coals broiling.

9. This morning we divided the dog into quarters, and he was dressed so neat, and being so fat
withall, that if I had seen him in a butcher's shop
I should have thought it to be a young lamb, and
good meat. We had a bag of potatoes given us,
to eat with our venison. Some stewed theirs ;
others roasted it; and I must confess, I made a tolerable meal out of some of this roasted dog, with
potatoes dipped in its drippings. Rats have been
eat in this prison often before. To-day the agent
told us that he had received an answer to our pe-

tition, and that we are to be allowed peas instead of greens, which is much better. He had received an order, that if we would deliver up those who were most active in digging the hole, the rest should be restored to full allowance. But the majority in prison were inclined to give them no satisfaction. This afternoon, however, two young men, of their own accord, went and delivered themselves up, and were sent to the Black-hole, thinking to live well, I suppose, while there, as doubtless they will.

10. To-day we were all restored to full allowance, and received peas. We had, also, white bread sent in by our friends. Thus, it is either a feast or a famine with us. I have been only eleven days on half allowance. To-day, about twelve o'clock, Mr. Heath sent a man to inform us that a cartel had arrived in Plymouth, for us. Soon after, Mr. Sorrey came with a letter which he had received from the committee in London, and read it to us, which informed us that one of the committee had waited on Lord Savage, the head lord of the Admiralty, to know the truth concerning this cartel, and he informed him that the Milford transport was engaged for that purpose, as a flag ship, and that we should be exchanged, one hundred at a time, and the first draft is to be from this prison, as we were committed first; so we

shall embark and proceed to Nantz, where they will take an equal number, and so go on till all the American prisoners in England are exchanged, if there be enough English prisoners in France that were taken by the Americans. There were only about forty or fifty committed before me, but as there have been upwards of one hundred who have lately attempted to escape from here, and most of them brought back, myself among the number ; and as it is customary in time of war for such to forfeit their turn, I began to despair of going in the first draft. In the mean time, all hands were called to hear a letter read, which the agent had received from the Lords of the Admiralty, who desired him to inform us that we were to be exchanged for the English prisoners in France, taken by the Americans ; and that, notwithstanding a number of us had attempted our escape, and by this means had forfeited our turn, yet, in this instance· we should be forgiven upon condition that we discovered through what corruption, or negligence, we effected our escape. This being read, he ordered the Black-hole doors to be opened. This is joyful news to us. Joy is to be seen on every man's countenance. This is a blessed day !

11. This afternoon Mr. Heath came to congratulate us on our prospect of deliverance, and

brought a letter with him, which informed us that the cartel is now in Plymouth, waiting only for a man to come from France to take charge of us.

12. To-day Mr. Sorrey came, and brought every man a sixpence, which is part of twenty pounds that has lately been sent down from London, and which was left of the old stock ; but we hear that they are about opening a new subscription.

13. We learn, from the papers, that the Spaniards have now seventy sail of the line, besides frigates and sloops, in different parts of Spain, mounting in all, seven thousand and three cannons, of different bores.

14. The sick, in the hospital, are most of them on the recovering order now, except three that moved down yesterday ; and to-night I am to go down and watch with them, as of late, since there has been so many sick, we have been allowed, two of a night, to go down and watch with them.

15. This afternoon a pardon came down from the King, for fifteen men in this prison, that petitioned last to go on board the men-of-war ; three of the number are already on board. They went out at the last hole, for that purpose. After the officers came to receive them, out of the twelve that remained in prison only four went, which makes forty-nine, in all, that have gone on board

the men-of-war from this prison ; besides numbers who have broke out and gone. It is astonishing to me, that men who have been used by the English as we have been, with all the severity that they have been masters of, should afterwards voluntarily enter their service.

16. Nothing remarkable.

17. Sunday. Nothing remarkable.

18. This forenoon, some officers from the ships came for some Frenchmen in the other yard, to carry them on board the men-of-war, and five out of the eight who would not go last Friday, altered their minds, and went, which makes fifty-four that have gone out of this yard, on board the men-of-war.

There are exactly two hundred and fifty American prisoners left here. This being the Queen's birth-day, the garrison and fort, and each ship in the harbor, in commission, fired twenty-one guns, as a royal salute.

19. We wait very impatiently for the man which we hear is to come from France to take charge of us. Though I am sensible he will make no unnecessary delays, yet he seems a long time coming ; so long, that some in prison begin to be doubtful whether he will come at all.

20. Some in prison, so far despair of a cartel,

that they have begun another hole. There was brought again, to-day, sixpence apiece for each man in prison.

21. Last night eleven Frenchmen made their escape from a separate prison, in another yard, and five soldiers are confined on the same account.

22. This forenoon Mr. Sorrey came again, and brought a couple of letters which he received from Bilboa, one of which was from Mr. Emery, of Bilboa, to Captain Lee's crew, which informed them that Captain Lee had arrived in Bilboa, and that his whole crew, if they would write, might be supplied with fifty shillings a share, and Captain Bradbury, in this prison, with six guineas.

This afternoon, all hands were called, and the agent called over the names of the hundred that were to go in the first draft, and desired that we should hold ourselves in readiness to be exchanged. Never was I so rejoiced to hear my name called, upon any occasion, as upon this. I am about the fortieth upon the agent's list. It appears that we are not to be exchanged as we were captured, but according to the date of our commitment, so that all our crew will not be included in the first draft. Out of one hundred and twenty which arrived in England, belonging to the Dolton, only eighty-six are left in prison to be exchanged.

23. We are so well assured of a cartel, now, that we lay aside all schemes for effecting our escape, and look out daily for orders to embark. An officer that belonged to the Mermaid frigate, that was chased ashore in America, who has been a prisoner in Philadelphia about a month, and has since been exchanged, and now arrived home, came to see us this afternoon, and talked with us. He gave us a very sad account of the price of provisions in America.

24. It is twenty-five months this night, that I have been a prisoner. We have been informed that last night, some men were discovered, in attempting to set fire to the King's dock-yard, in this port.

25. There are seven or eight now in the hospital, sick with fevers, but most of them are upon the recovering order, except those who were lately taken sick, two of which number labor under great concern of mind, relating to their future state, and to-day we obtained liberty of Mr. Coudry, to send for a minister.

26. It is two years and two months, to-day, since I sailed from Portsmouth, in the brig Dolton.

27. Nothing remarkable.

28. As to-morrow is port day, we put great dependence on it, expecting an order from London concerning our exchange.

29. This morning Mr. Sorrey brought each of us another sixpence, which balances the twenty pounds before mentioned ; and two of our officers, as usual, went up into the agent's office, to receive the money. The agent showed them a letter which he had received from London, with a pardon from the King for the first hundred that is to be exchanged.

30. Nothing remarkable.

31. Sunday. This is port day again, and there is no news for us to-day. It was a week last Friday since we were told to hold ourselves in readiness to be exchanged, and no signs of a cartel appears. If Job himself was here, his patience would be worn out.

CHAPTER XXII.

John Foster, Elias Vickey, and Asa Witham died — Mr. Deal's
    Escape — Effect of long Imprisonment — New Subscription — Mil-
    ford Transport — Joyful News — Hole Discovered — Keppel Ac-
    quitted — Bonfires — Escape — No Coals in Plymouth — Excite-
    ment about the Dog — Love to Friends — James Valentine died —
    Bills of Exchange from Bilboa — Cartel Arrives — Lieutenant Knox
    Arrives — Leaves the Prison — Kind Usage on Cartel — Bonner
    Darling died

FEBRUARY 1. This morning about three o'clock,
Mr. John Foster died in the prison hospital, of a
nervous fever. Some of Mr. Foster's townsmen
were of a mind that he should be buried in a white
linen shirt, but they received for an answer, that
no person in this country was allowed to be buried
in any thing but sheep's clothing. The American
prisoners, who died in the royal hospitals, were
buried in black, but very rough coffins; but those
who die in prison are buried in a rough white
coffin. This Mr. Foster is the eighth man that has
died since I came to prison — the seventh man

of our crew that has died since we have been taken, and the seventeenth American prisoner that has died in prison and in the royal hospital, since we were captured.

2. To-day a gentleman came here, whom we are informed is but fourteen days from Dunkirk, but last from London, and he brought a letter from the Board, which ordered the agent to let him inspect every thing which he had a mind to. He looked at our meat, weighed our bread, and tasted our beef, and we are told that he has been in every prison in France.

3. This morning about five o'clock, Elias Vickery died. He was a Marblehead man. He was taken in one of the Freedom's prizes; and about six o'clock, Asa Witham died. He belongs to New Gloucester, and was taken in the Dolton. They have both been sick upwards of twelve months. — They make ten in number that have died since I have been in prison, and eight of our crew since we have been taken, and nineteen in all that have died of different crews since we have been taken. Last evening Mr. Deal made his escape from the officers' prison.

4. Three men have died this week, and there are sixteen or eighteen now sick. Of late, every day more or less are taken sick, and most of them with fever. Yesterday a French frigate, of twen-

ty-six guns, was brought in here, which was taken by an English frigate.

5. This is another port day, and no news for us, concerning a cartel. It is unaccountable to me that it is so long coming. It is twenty months to-day, since I entered this prison.

6. It is so long since we heard of a cartel that the greater part in prison begin to despair of its coming. Many of those in prison are like so many children; as long as a rattle is ringing in their ears, they are quiet and easy, but as soon as the rattle stops, they are faithless and impatient.

We have another hole in hand, which will take us nearly a month to complete; so that if this news proves abortive, we may have recourse to another way.

Last evening a man made his escape over the wall, but before any one could get out, it was discovered.

7. This is another port day, and no news for us.

8. Nothing remarkable.

9. This afternoon Mr. Sorrey sent us sixpence apiece to each man in prison, which we are informed, is part of a new subscription which is opened.

10. Yesterday was port day, and this morning the agent informed us that His Majesty had been

graciously pleased to pardon one hundred of us, in order for an exchange; and that he had received an order from the Board of Commissioners of sick and wounded seamen, to deliver one hundred of us to Lieutenant Knox, whenever he should call for us. This Lieutenant Knox is to command the Milford transport, which is the cartel.

> Transporting news ! who can tell,
> The joy that doth this joy excell ;
> Long as we live we should adore
> The goodness God lays up in store.

11. We have been informed that the cartel is in Portsmouth, and never heard to the contrary, until to-day, when the agent informed us that she is in Dartmouth, waiting only for a fair wind to come down the channel.

12. Nothing remarkable.

13. Nothing transpired worthy of notice.

14. Through some dirt that was laid about the prison, and discovered by the turnkeys, which gave them cause to suspect we had another hole in hand, the guard came in, and after a long search, found it.

15. It is two years and three months since I sailed in the brig Dolton, from Newbury.

16. Nothing remarkable.

17. Last night two men made their escape from

the officers prison, but were taken up and brought back to-day. Last night, Plymouth was illuminated on account of Admiral Keppel being acquitted with honor.

18. The wind is to the eastward to-day, but no signs of a cartel appears.

19. Upon a large hill, a little distance from the prison, we see a couple of flag-staffs erected, but we know not the occasion of it.

20. Upon the same hill where the flag-staffs were erected yesterday, there were two large bonfires last night, and the houses all around illuminated, which, we are told, was on account of the plot being discovered against the King's dock-yard, and last night was the time it was to be put into execution.

21. Nothing remarkable.

24. Last night a man made his escape out of this prison, by getting over the wall. This morning Mr. Sorrey came, and brought each of us another sixpence. For a few days past, we have had no coals to burn. Mr. Sorrey informed us that a bushel of coal is not to be purchased in Plymouth, at any price. He also informed us that fourteen sail of vessels, laden with coal, had lately been taken, bound from Newcastle. This afternoon, also, Mr. Heath came to see us; he has lately returned from London. He read a letter to us,

which informed us that the cartel is in the Downs, detained only by contrary winds; also, that there has been a great talk in London, concerning our eating a dog, and that it had been published in the papers, and he desired that we would let him know the truth of it, whether we eat it from actual necessity or not. Mr. Heath sent us some soap and tobacco.

25. This forenoon, a gentleman came to see us, who is lately from London. He told us that when he sailed, the cartel absolutely lay in the Downs. By this time I hope we have got the truth of it.

26. Yesterday three gentlemen, who are our friends, came with Mr. Heath to see us. We have been so long confined, that when a friend comes into the yard to see us, we flock around him like children, and love the ground he treads upon. Also, to-day, we wrote them out the facts relating to the dog, agreeably to their request.

27. Nothing of interest.

28. Sunday. The wind hauls round to the northward and eastward, which gives us now to hope that our cartel will be here in a few days.

March 1. Nothing remarkable.

2. Nothing worthy of notice.

3. We understand that there is a fleet bound to the East Indies, and another to the West Indies,

that lay wind-bound, up channel, as well as our cartel.

4. This morning, James Valentine died with a fever. He was a Marblehead man, and belonged to Captain Lee's crew. He is the twentieth man that has died since I have been taken, and the eleventh since I have been in prison. This has been a fast day with us; for the beef that came in this morning was so bad, and so far from being according to contract, that we sent it back again.— The second that came, was worse than the first, and we refused it, also. Our peas are also bad, so that we could not eat them, and by applying to the officer of the guard, who spoke in our behalf, we received cheese instead of beef, but not until evening.

5. This morning we received the joyful tidings that our cartel had arrived. Some of the Marblehead men received letters from home, by way of a vessel that was taken. The bills of exchange for one hundred and nine pounds sterling, have arrived from Bilboa, for Captain Lee's crew, and are sent to London to be answered.

6. Notwithstanding our cartel has arrived, we understand that she is to wait for orders from London, before she can embark us.

7. Nothing remarkable.

8. This forenoon the outward bound East India fleet, with their convoys, passed by this port.

9. Nothing of interest.

10. This morning Lieutenant Knox, who is to transact the business of our exchange, came to see us, and informed us that he expects to embark us the beginning of next week. The cartel has come up to Stonehouse creek, where we can see her from the prison.

11. Nothing remarkable.

12. The wind has now veered round to the southward, and blows up rain, which I fear will delay our going.

13. This afternoon the agent, Mr. Coudry, informed us that on Monday, at ten o'clock, we are to embark.

14. Sunday. We are so impatient to be gone, that every moment of this day seems an hour long.

15. It is two years and four months to-day, since I left Newbury. This forenoon, about eleven o'clock, ninety-seven of us in number, were guarded down, and embarked on board the cartel — two of our number having died since we received the King's pardon, and one being dangerously ill.

16. We are now on board the cartel, and waiting only for a fair wind to sail. We are allowed the liberty of the deck, by day and night, and we

have tolerable good accommodations.   We lodge
in cabins; most of us have beds of our own, and
those who have not, have King's bedding.   There
are three or four sick amongst us, and they have
single cabins by themselves.   To-day we had salt
beef and pudding, which is a great rarity.

17. The wind is still against us, but I feel much
easier here than I should be in prison. Here we have
a change of diet, though it is no more than prisoners' allowance, and both officers and men behave
very civil to us.

18. To-day Mr. Heath came on board, and another of our friends, and brought some wine, tea,
and sugar, and other necessaries, for those who
are sick.

19. To-day the prison doctor came on board,
and informed us that Bonner Darling is dead — a
negro man that belonged to Marblehead, and one
of our crew.   He makes twenty-one that have died
since I have been taken; and nine of the number
were of the Dolton's company.

CHAPTER XXIII.

Journal Lost — Thirty enter with Jones — Joins the Alliance — Arrive at L' Orient with Prize — Second Cruise — Journal Lost — Extracts from Paul Jones' Life — At Dr. Franklin's House — Joins again the Alliance — Sails Home.

[The journal of their passage to France is lost. The next record that is preserved, presents Mr. Herbert to us at Nantes, situated on the river Loire, in the south-western part of France.]

April 12. We lay here under pay, from the 5th of this month; have our board paid, and have nothing to do but walk about town. I have tried, but can get no labor, as business is very much stagnated here. Nearly forty sail of merchantmen are hauled up, and lay idle in this port.

14. About forty of our men have entered with Captain Jones, for twelve months, and this morning they set out for L' Orient, about seventy-five miles distant, by land.

17. Yesterday and to-day, I have been at work on board the Pallas, a French ship. To-day, the Alliance arrived here, with prisoners to be exchanged for us.

28. This day I received from Mr. Odaire, sixteen livres, which, including the four crowns before received, amounts to forty livres, which is a month's pay.

30. This day we embarked on board the Alliance.*

May 16. This day we sailed for L' Orient.†

---

* The Alliance is said by Commodore Jones to have been so called, for the following reasons:

" When the treaty of alliance with France arrived in America, Congress, feeling the most lively sentiments of gratitude towards France, thought how they might manifest the satisfaction of the Country by some public act. The finest frigate in the service was on the stocks, ready to be launched, and it was resolved to call her the Alliance."

† Extract from correspondence of Dr. Franklin, at this time, throwing light upon the journal of Mr. Herbert:

Passy, June 26th, 1779.

Dr. Franklin from the Committee on Foreign Affairs.

GENTLEMEN,

The Marquis de Lafayette, who arrived here on the 11th of February, brought me yours of October 28th, and the new commission, credentials, and instructions, the Congress have honored me with.

June 19. This day we sailed from L' Orient, on a cruize in company with Captain Jones, a French frigate, a brig and a cutter.*

I immediately acquainted the minister of foreign affairs with my appointment, and communicated to him, as is usual, a copy of my credential letter, on which a day was named for my reception. The end of that part of the instructions, which relates to American seamen taken by the French in English ships, had already been obtained; Captain Jones having had for some time, an order from court, directed to the keepers of the prisoners, requiring them to deliver to him such Americans as should be found in their hands, that they might be at liberty to serve under his command. Most of them, if not all, have been delivered to him. The minister of marine requesting that the Alliance might be added to Commodore Jones' little squadron, and offering to give Mr. Adams a passage in the frigate, with the new ambassador, I thought it best to continue her a little longer in Europe, hoping she may, in the projected cruize, by her extraordinary swiftness, be a means of taking prisoners enough to redeem the rest of our countrymen now in the English jails. With this view, I ordered her to join Captain Jones, at L' Orient, and obey his orders, where she is now, accordingly.

* [From Paul Jones to Dr. Franklin.]

On board the Bon homme Richard, at anchor,
Isle of Groaix, off L' Orient, July 1st, 1779.
His Excellency Benjamin Franklin.

HONORED AND DEAR SIR,

On the 19th ult., the American squadron under my

June 20. Last night, precisely at 12 o'clock,
just as the starboard watch was going on deck, it
was very pleasant weather, and we were lying to,
with our topsails back to the masts. Captain Jones
came down before the wind and run us down upon
our 'starboard quarter, carrying away our mizen-
mast, and doing us much damage, and himself
more, by springing his bowsprit, carrying away his
head and cut-water, but fortunately no one was
killed on board either of the ships.

---

command, consisting of the Bon homme Richard, 42
guns, Alliance, 36 guns, Pallas, 30 guns, Cerf, 18 guns,
and the Vengeance, 12 guns, sailed from hence with a
convoy of merchant ships and transports with troops,
&c., bound to the different ports and garrisons between
this place and Bordeaux.

On the evening of the following day, I had the satisfaction to see the latter part of the convoy safe within
the entrance of the river of Bordeaux, the rest having
been safely escorted into the entrance of Nantz, Roche-
fort, &c.   But at the preceding midnight, while lying-to
off Isle of Vew, the Bon homme Richard and Alliance
got foul of one another, and carried away the head and
cut-water, sprit-sail yard, and jib-boom of the former,
with the mizen-mast of the latter; fortunately, however,
neither received damage in the hull.   In the evening
of the 21st, I sent the Cerf to reconnoitre two sail, and
Captain Varage was so ardent in the pursuit, that he

had lost sight of the squadron next morning; and I am now told, that he had a warm engagement with one of them, a sloop of 14 guns, which he took, but was obliged to abandon, on the approach of another enemy of superior force. The action lasted an hour and a half; several men were killed and wounded on board the Cerf. That cutter is now fitting at L' Orient. On the 22d we had a rencontre with three ships of war. They were to windward, and bore down in a line abreast for some time, but seeing we were prepared to receive them, they hauled their wind, and by carrying a press of sail got clear, in spite of our utmost endeavors to bring them to action. On the 26th, we lost company of the Alliance and Pallas. I am unable to say where the blame lays. I gave the ships a rendezvous off Penmark rocks, but did not meet them there.

I anchored here yesterday noon, having had a rencontre the night before with two of the enemy's ships of war in the offing, in the sight of this island and Belle Isle. Previous to this I had given the Vengeance leave to make the best of her way to this road, so that the enemy found me alone in a place where I had no expectation of a hostile visit. They appeared at first earnest to engage, but their courage failed, and they fled with precipitation, and to my mortification out-sailed the Bon homme Richard and got clear. I had, however, a flattering proof of the martial spirit of my crew, and I am confident, that had I been able to get between the two, which was my intention, we should have beaten them both together.

July 2. We arrived at L' Orient, after a cruize of thirteen days ; likewise, the prize brig, which we took on the 28th of June, from Bordeaux bound to Dublin, with five hundred and sixty casks of wine and brandy on board.*

August 14. Having repaired our ships, and got a clean bottom, we sailed this day for L' Orient on a cruise with Captain Jones, two French frigates, two brigs, and a cutter. With this fleet we made the best of our way to Ireland. On our passage, we took in company a ship ; soon after, Captain Jones took a brig laden with provisions. A few days after, we made Ireland. Upon making land, Captain Jones took a brig from Newfoundland, laden with oil and blubber, and after cruizing a few days along shore, we parted from the fleet in a gale of wind.

---

* [Dr. Franklin to Paul Jones.]

I can say nothing about Captain Landais' prize. I suppose the minister has an account of it, but I have heard nothing from him about it. If he reclaims it on account of his passport, we must then consider what is . to be done. I approve of the careenage proposed for the Alliance, as a thing necessary. As she is said to be a remarkable swift sailer, I should hope you might by her means take some privateers and a number of prisoners, so as to continue the cartel, and redeem all our poor countrymen.

[Here some pages of the journal are lost, but the journal of Captain Jones will supply its place.]

[From Paul Jones to Dr. Franklin.]

On board the ship Serapis, at anchor without } the Texel, in Holland, Oct. 3d, 1779. {

His Excellency Benjamin Franklin.

HONORED AND DEAR SIR,

When I had the honor of writing to you on the 11th of August, previous to my departure from the Road of Groaix, I had before me the most flattering prospect of rendering essential service to the common cause of France and America. I had a full confidence in the voluntary inclination and ability of every captain under my command to assist and support me in my duty with cheerful emulation ; and I was pursuaded that every one of them would pursue glory in preference to interest.

Whether I was, or was not deceived, will best appear by a relation of circumstances.

The little squadron under my orders, consisting of the Bon homme Richard, of 40 guns, the Alliance, of 36 guns, the Pallas, of 32 guns, the Cerf, of 18 guns, and the Vengeance, of 12 guns, joined by two privateers, the Monsieur and the Granville, sailed from the Road of Groaix at day-break on the 14th of August.

The evening of the 26th brought with it stormy weather, with the appearance of a severe gale from the S. W. The gale continued to increase in the night, with thick weather. To prevent separation, I carried a top-light, and fired a gun every quarter of an hour. I carried, al-

21

so, very moderate sail, and the course had already been
clearly pointed out before night, yet with all this precau-
tion, I found myself accompanied only by the brigantine
Vengeance in the morning, the Granville having remained astern with a prize.   As I have since under-
stood, the tiller of the Pallas broke, after midnight,
which disabled her from keeping up, but no apology
has yet been made on behalf of the Alliance.

On the 31st, we saw the Flamie Islands situated near
the Lewis, on the N. W. coast of Scotland; and the
next morning, off Cape Wrath, we gave chase to a ship
to windward; at the same time two ships appeared in the
N. W. quarter, which proved to be the Alliance and
a prize ship which she had taken, bound, as I understand,
from Liverpool to Jamaica.   The ship which I chased
brought too at noon; she proved to be the Union letter
of marque, bound from London to Quebec, with a car-
go of naval stores on account of government, adapted
for the service of the British armed vessels on the lakes.
The public despatches were lost, as the Alliance very
imprudently hoisted American colors, though English
colors were then flying on board the Bon homme Richard.   Captain Landais sent a small boat to ask whether
I would man the ship or he should, as in the latter case
he would suffer no boat nor person from the Bon homme
Richard to go near the prize.   Ridiculous as this appeared to me, I yielded to it for the sake of peace, and
received the prisoners on board the Bon homme Richard, while the prize was manned from the Alliance.

On the morning of the 4th, the Alliance appeared
again, and had brought too two very small coasting

sloops, in ballast, but without having attended properly to my orders of yesterday. The Vengeance joined me soon after, and informed me that in consequence of Captain Landais' orders to the commanders of the two prize ships, they had refused to follow him to the rendezvous. I am at this moment ignorant of what orders these men received from Captain Landais, nor know I by virtue of what authority he ventured to give his orders to prizes in my presence, and without either my orders or approbation.

Two rich Letters of Marque were taken off the coast of Scotland, and Captain Landais took upon himself, even under my very nose, and without my knowledge, to order them to Bergen, in Norway, where they were given up to the English.—*Paul Jones to the Board of Admiralty.*

Three of their prizes sent into Bergen, in Norway, were, at the instance of the British minister, seized by order of the court of Denmark, and delivered up to him. —*Letter from Dr. Franklin to Samuel Huntington, Esq. President of Congress.*

The following letter from Dr. Franklin to Paul Jones, shows the value of those prizes, taken and delivered up as above. There can be no doubt that Mr. Herbert was sent in one of the above prizes, as the next entry in his journal is from Bergen, in Norway.

Havre, July 21st, 1785.

The Hon. Paul Jones.

DEAR SIR,—The offer of which you desire I would give you the particulars, was made to me by M. le Baron de Waltersdorff, in behalf of His Majesty the King of Denmark, by whose ministers he said he was authorised to make it. It was to give the sum of ten thousand pounds sterling, as a compensation for having delivered up the prizes to the English. I did not accept it, conceiving it much too small a sum, they having been valued to me at sixty thousand pounds. I wrote to Mr. Hodgson, an insurer in London, requesting he would procure information of the sums insured on those Canada ships. His answer was, that he could find no traces of such insurance, and he believed none was made, for the government, on whose account they were said to be loaded with military stores, never insured.— But, by the best judgment he could make, he thought they might be worth about sixteen or eighteen thousand pounds each.

———

By the following letter it will be seen that Bergen was one of the places designated by Dr. Franklin, for sending prizes to.

Passy, June 30th, 1779.

Hon. Captain Jones.

DEAR SIR,—The prizes you may make, send to Dunkirk, Ostend, or Bergen, in Norway, according to your proximity to either of those ports.

February 5th, 1780. This day our officers received a letter from France, from a gentleman in Paris, which informs us that the King of Denmark is to pay for the prizes we brought in here, fifty thousand pounds stirling, which is two hundred and fifty thousand Rix dollars. He is likewise to pay all our expenses while here. We likewise received orders to repair to Dunkirk as quick as possible, but we are to have a pass from the King of Denmark, which is what we wait for.

8. This day I received a pair of shoes, in balance of four shillings due me as wages.

25. This day I received half a guinea of a Scotchman, for which I gave him eleven shillings.

March 4. This morning arrived here from Virginia, a ship laden with tobacco, under French colors.

18. Fortunately I have got another guinea for which I paid only twenty-one shillings.

21. This day I received a pair of shoes, at five shillings.

April 1. I have received one shilling and sixpence for repairing shoes.

5. This day I received of Captain Thomas White, in behalf of wages due, four Rix dollars, each valued at four shillings stirling.

I have worked several days on board the before-

mentioned tobacco ship, and have likewise made
some chests for the seamen, for all of which I received four dollars.

10. This day I received of Captain Thomas
White, two pounds six shillings and sevenpence
halfpenny, stirling, which was the ballance due me
for clothing which I was charged with, but did not
receive — all of which was given by the King of
Denmark.   The occasion of this was, that when
we were turned on shore, many of our men were
in want of clothing.   Our officers interceded for
them, and procured the amount of four pounds
four shillings sterling each ; and as I received only
a trifle in clothing, I received the remainder in
money.

11. This day we embarked on board a gallion,
of about seventy tons, found and provisioned by
the King of Denmark, to carry us to Dunkirk,
after boarding us here nearly six months.

19. This day we sailed from Bergen, after being
there seven months and five days.

May 4. We arrived at Dunkirk, after a passage of seventeen days.

5. To-day I received of Captain Thomas
White, forty livres, in behalf of wages due.

16. We set out to travel to Paris, which is
one hundred and eighty miles, having a wagon
to carry our baggage, and received eighteen livres

per man, of Mr. Coffin, the American agent in Flanders, to bear our expenses to Paris.

21. This day, about eight o'clock in the morning, we arrived in the city of Paris, after a pleasant journey of more than three days, through Flanders into France and Paris. After we arrived at Paris we put up our horses, and stopped not either to eat or to drink, but made the best of our way to Passy, about four miles from Paris, where Dr. Franklin resides. After we came to Dr. Franklin's house and had a little conversation with him, he ordered his servants to get us breakfast, which we eat in his house, and likewise dinner. The Dr. sent his servants to provide lodgings for us, which he could not procure, on account of the King and Queen, and all the nobility, being in town, and all the public houses being taken up; therefore we carried our luggage to Dr. Franklin's house, where we were well entertained ; and here we saw Mr. Adams and Mr. Dean. We procured lodgings for ourselves in the afternoon. The gentleman who owns the house where Dr. Franklin resides, ordered one of his servants to show us his gardens, to guide us through the town, and show us the King and Queen and all the nobility ; these we have seen twice to-day, as they passed through the town, besides many other curious objects, both in Paris and Passy.

23. To-day our board was paid, and we received two guineas to bear our expenses to L' Orient, which is three hundred and sixty miles, and likewise a pass.* We shall be obliged to travel on foot; therefore I am compelled to sell, or give away, all my clothing, except a trifle of the best, which I shall retain as a change.

24. This day we commenced our journey to L' Orient.

June 5. We arrived at L' Orient.

7. To-day I went on board the Alliance.

8. We sailed in the Alliance for America, in company with a ship, a brig, a schooner and a lugger. Also, I received this day of the purser, on board the Alliance, two shirts, one pair of shoes, a pair of trousers and a knife.

July 10. This day I received of the purser, one outside jacket.

August 13. We made land, which proved to be Cape Ann, having a passage of thirty-eight days, from land to land.

I left the Alliance, August 21st, and arrived home at Newbury, August 23d, 1780.

---

* The widow of Mr. Herbert has now in her possession a crown piece, which her husband received of Dr. Franklin, at this time.

LIST OF PRISONERS TAKEN IN THE BRIG-ANTINE DOLTON, AND COMMITTED TO MILL PRISON, PLYMOUTH, ENGLAND, JUNE, 1777.

The following marks denote (*) dead — (†) escaped — (‡) joined English men-of-war — (§) died or escaped before any were committed to prison — (P. J.) means with Paul Jones — (A.) in the Alliance.

Captain Eleazer Johnston † Newburyport, Mass.
1st Lieut. Anthony Knapp † "
2d Lieut. John Buntin "
Daniel Lunt † "
Alexander Ross † "
Offin Boardman † "
Moses Cross "
Thomas Cluston † "
Cutting Lunt (P. J.) "
Wym'd. Bradbury "
Henry Lunt (P. J.) "
Samuel Cutler † "
Francis Little "
Joseph Asulier † "
Joseph Brewster (P. J.) "
Nathaniel Wyer † "
John Knowlton § "
Joseph Racklief "
William Shackford (A.) "
John Key † "
John Barrenger † "
—— Stickney "

Joseph Poor (A.)   Newburyport, Mass.
Nathaniel Warner   "
Josiah George †   "
Moses Merrill   "
Jacob True (P. J.)   "
John George   "
Richard Lunt (A.)   "
Ebenezer Brown (A.)   "
Paul Noyes (A.)   "
Joseph Plummer (A.)   "
Reuben Tucker   "
John Smith (A.)   "
Charles Herbert (A.)   "
Joseph Choate (A.)   "
Thomas Bayley (A.)   "
Nathaniel Bayley (P. J.)   "
Benjamin Carr (A.)   "
Samuel Woodbridge   "
Henry Smith   "
Ebenzer Edwards (A.)   "
Jonathan Whitmore ‡   "
Edward Spooner ‡   "
Daniel Cottle *   "
Ebenezer Hunt *   "
Asa Witham *   New Gloucester.
Zebulon Davis   "
Daniel Lane †   "
Benjamin Yolin (A.)   "
Nathaniel Marshall   Portsmouth.
Benjamin C. Stubbs   "
Jacob Nutter   "
George Triffering   "
Benjamin Babb †   "
John Abbot ‡   "

Joseph Shilaby (A.)   Portsmouth.
Guppy Studley   "
Samuel Stacey (P. J.)   Kittery, N. H.
Joshua Casual   "
John Foster *   "
Hugh Kenniston †   "
Peter Tobey   "
John Perkins   "
William Lewis   "
Richard Sowards   "
Nathaniel Kennard (P. J.)   "
Stephen Lawley   "
Samuel Fletcher (P. J.)   "
Thomas Mahoney (P. J.)   "
Winthrop Willey   "
Jacob Brewer   "
Daniel Knight (A.)   "
Nathaniel Staples   "
George Fernel   "
Ephraim Clark (A.)   "
John Gunnison (P. J.)   "
Samuel Scriggins *   "
Tobias Weymouth,   Berwick, N. H.
Gideon Warren *   "
Thomas Hammet (P. J.)   "
Thomas Rines *   "
Ebenezer Libbey   "
Ichabod Lord (P. J.)   "
Aaron Goodwin   "
John Higgins   "
Andrew Whittam   "
James Sellers,   Old York, N. H.
Tobias Sellers   "
Timothy Harris   "

John Downs (P. J.)   Old York, N. H.
John Simpson (A.)   Windham.
Andrew Templeton   "
John Burbank (P. J.)   Cape Porpoise.
Israel Lasèdel   "
William Maxwell,   Block Point.
Samuel Carroll (A.)   "
John Maddon (P. J.)   "
Joseph Burnham   "
Samuel Smith   "
Joseph Clark, ‡   Boston, Mass.
John Bass ‡   "
Robert Burgoyne †   "
Joseph Hatch *   "
Nathaniel Porter, Cape Pursue.
Jacob Wyman   "
Dr. Samuel Smith, †   Hampton.
Elisha Johnston   "
Ichabod Shaw   "
James Lawrence, Salem.
Henry Barrett, † Ireland.
William Smith ‡   "
William Horner ‡   "
Adam Ladley, † Scotland.
Clement Woodhouse, † England.
William Ford, ‡ Virginia.
John McCoffrey, Casco Bay.
Isaac Leajor   "
Bonner Darling, * Marblehead.

ROLL OF MILL PRISON, PLYMOUTH, ENG-
LAND, FEBRUARY 7, 1779.

Sloop Charming Sally, taken January 16th, 1777.

Captain Francis Brown,† New Haven.
Refiter Griffin,   . "   "
Jonathan Hodgcare,   "   "
William Woodward,†   "   "
Anthony Shomaker,† Long Island.
William Keys,   "   "
Benjamin Powers, Millbury.
Arthur Bennett,   "
Isaac George,
Kirtland Griffin, Gilford.
Henry Wrightinton, Dartmouth.
Samuel Knast,   "
John Hathaway,   "
James Bounds,   "
William Cuff,   "
Prince Hall ‡   "
Humphry Potter ‡   "
Ebenezer Willis *   "
Absalom Nero *
Thomas Brightman,   "
Silas Hathaway,   "

Joseph Fredrick, Martha's Vineyard.
Thomas Chase,   "   "
Jeremiah Luce,   "   "
Thomas Luce   "   "
Abisha Rogers,   "   "
Barzilla Crowell,   "   "
Samuel Lambert   "   "
Manuel Swasey,   "   "
John Lot *   "   "
Cuff Scott ‡   "   "
William Harden §   "   "
Eliphalet Rogers,   "   "
James Dean, ‡ Hartford,
Jacob Norris, Carolina.
Alexander Frazier, ‡ New York.
William Black,   "   "
Henry Sheaf †   "   "
Phineas Smith †   "   "
William Vanderson ‡ "   "
William Andrews, ‡ Ireland.
Thomas Welch ‡   "   '
Bartley Barrell ‡   "
Benjamin Shakle, * England.
William Creper ‡   "
Francis Kirtland ‡   "
William Carpenter ‡   "
William Asburn ‡   "
John George Stamfield, ‡ Holland.
John Daghan ‡   "
Robert Richey, ‡ Scotland.
James Judson *   "

Lexington Prize, taken April, 1777. — Committed to prison June, 1777.

Nicholas Simpkin, * Jersey.
William Stearns, Maryland.
Thomas Haley, England.
Benjamin Locket ‡   "
William Lane, Philadelphia.
John Gordon, ‡ Ireland.

Brigantine Fancy, taken August 7th, 1777.

Captain John Lee, † Newburyport.
Daniel Lane,   "
John Bickford,   "
William White,   "
Francis Salter, † Marblehead.
William Laskey,   "
Joseph Barker †   "
Thomas Barker †   "
Richard Goss,   "
Nicholas Thorn,   "
Samuel Beal,   "
John Lio,   "
James Fox,   "
Thomas Mack †   "
Robert Swan †   "
John Swan †   "
Jonathan Bartlett,   "
Samuel Hawley,   "
Jacob Vickery,   "
Nicholas Gardner,   "

James Valentine, * Marblehead.
John Crow,   "
Elias Hart *   "
William Pickett,   "
Robert Pierce,   "
Robert Brown,   "
Skillings Brooks,   "
Thomas Horton,   "
William Cole,   "
Jacob Vickery, Jr,   "
John Adams,   "
Edmund Baden,   "
Samuel Whitrong,   "
Benjamin Masten,   "
Michael Treffrey,   "
Andrew Slyfield †   "
Cæsar Bartlett, Ipswich.
Samuel Treadwell,   "
Nathaniel Jones,   "
Samuel Harris,   "
Samuel Latham,   "
William Longfellow, "
Adams Choate,   "
Daniel Goodhue,   "
John Fowler *   "
Charles Barnes,   "
Joseph Fisher, Doct., † "
William Lir, Sweden.
Alex. Baxter, England.
Luke Larcomb,   "
Israel Matthews, "

Wm. Skinner, †   England.
Martin Shaw,   "
Robert Stevenson, Scotland.
Thomas Salter,   "

Brigantine Freedom's Prize, taken April 27th, 1777.

John Demond,   Marblehead.
Stephen Demise,   "
Thomas Brown †   "
Joseph Striker,   "
Joseph Magery,   "
Elias Vickery,   "
William Brown,   "
Nathaniel Stacey, † "
James Lyon,   "
Jacob Lord, †   "
Christian Codrer,   "

Ship Reprisal's Prize, taken June 29th, 1777. — Committed in August.

Thomas Norwood, † Bristol.
Samuel Ross,   "
Stafford Badan, Virginia.
Alex. Knell, ‡   "
Thomas Driver, Ireland.
Charles Kneet, Baltimore.
Thomas Runnells, ‡ "
Edwin Lewis, ‡ Philadelphia.
Daniel Acham, † Virginia.
Joseph McMullen, Ireland.

Sloop Hawk's Prize, taken April 13th, 1778. — Committed in October, 1778.

John Picknall,   Salem.
John Haynes,   "
John Deadman,   "
John Foy,   "
Wood Abrahams, "
English Thomas, Boston.

Schooner Hawk's Prize, taken September 18th, 1777. — Committed October 16th.

Benjamin Leech, Manchester.
Abial Lee,   "
Moses Stacey, Marblehead.
Thomas Wigger,   "
Thomas Knowlton.
Amherst Weight.

Brigantine Lexington, taken September 19th, 1779

Captain Henry Johnston, † Boston.
David Welch, † Ireland.
Arthur Kirk †   "
John Kennedy ‡   "
Thos. Choulston ‡ "
John Hopes,   "
William Lee,   "
Robert Ford,   "
William Riley,   "
Phil. McLoughlan, "
James Haze ‡   "

Thomas Bradley, Ireland.
John Barry †   "
James Dick,   "
Joseph Coulston ‡   "
Jonn Howard ‡   "
Thomas Welch ‡   "
Nicholas Chaise ‡   "
Thomas Marley ‡   "
Nath'l. Brennon ‡   "
Andrew Grace, ‡   Philadelphia.
James Shields ‡   "
Daniel Fagan ‡   "
Jacob Crawford,   "
Thomas Harvey,   "
Francis Colburn ‡   "
David Clark ‡   "
Henry Bakeley ‡   "
Richard Deal, †   Virginia.
Henry Lawrence,   "
George Thayer,   Providence.
John Chester,   England.
Thomas Lines ‡   "
Matthew Clear ‡   "
John Videan ‡   "
Samuel Williams ‡   "
John Davis ‡   "
Joseph Wolt ‡   "
Benj'n. Richardson ‡   "
Edward Hart ‡   "
George Morrison,   Scotland.
Joseph Kennigton *   "

John Stewart, ‡ Scotland.
Samuel Hobble, New London.
Aaron Twigley, ‡ New Jersey.

Schooner Warren, taken December 29th, 1777. — Committed June, 1778.

Captain John Ravel, †   Salem.
Samuel Foote,   "
John Battan,   "
——— Smith,   "
——— Lander,   "
Benjamin Bickett,   "
Thomas Manning,   "
Joseph Lambert,   "
Stephen Waters,   "
Jonathan Archer,   "
John Jones,   "
William Bright ‡   "
Josiah Jordon,   "
Clifford Crowningfield, "
Edward Yoling,   "
Peter Harris,   "
Thomas Majory,   "
Samuel Townsend,   "
Daniel Chubb,   "
Richard Crispin,   "
Samuel Knapp,   "
John Underwood,   "
Nathaniel Ward,   "
John Batten, Jr.,   "
Thomas Stephens,   "

William Archer, ‡ Salem. .

Benjamin Chipman, Beverly.

John Cushing, Doct., Haverhill.

Eben Bosworth, Bristol.

Sampson Simms, Bristol.

Thomas Austin, Rhode Island.

Samuel Harris,   "

William Clark,   "

Edward Sisal,   "

William Race, ‡ Philadelphia.

John Phillips †   "

Peter Merry,   "

Joseph Ingersoll, ‡ Cape Ann.

Robert McCleary, ‡ Boston.

Ezekiel Canny, ‡ Carolina.

*Schooner Black Snake, taken August 16th, 1777. —
Committed March 12th, 1778.*

Captain William Lucran, Marblehead.

John Wheeler, Rhode Island.

John Buckley, North Carolina.

Ship Oliver Cromwell, taken May 19th, 1777. — Committed October 18th, 1777.

Patrick McCann, Ireland.

John Dority,   "

James Lawny ‡   "

John Adair,   "

Richard Price, Maryland.

William Hall, ‡ New Jersey.

George Still, † England. .

Letter of Marque Janey, taken May 24th. — Committed
August 19th.

Captain George Rolls,† Virginia.
George Watkins,   "

Brigantine Cabot's Prize, taken October 24th, 1776. —
Committed June, 1777.

Peter Cassenbury, Philadelphia,
Paul Magee, Rhode Island.
David Covel, Virginia.

True Blue, taken January 3d. — Committed August
20th, 1778.

Peter Janes, Marblehead.

Brigantine Ranger's Prize, taken August 23d, 1778.
Charles Sherman, Rhole Island.

Merchantman Sweet Lucretia, taken July 5th. — Com-
mitted October 16th, 1778.

James Horton, Casco Bay.
Samuel Lewis, Boston.

Schooner Musquito, taken and committed.
William Dayton, ‡ St. Martin's.
Captain John Martin, ‡ England.
William Morris †   "

Sturdy Beggar's Prize, taken October, 1776. — Committed June, 1777.

George Southard, Salem.
Philip Misseroy, Marblehead.
James Richardson,   "

Revenge's Prize, taken August 2d.

William Hessam, Philadelphia.
William Fowler, Casco Bay.
Daniel Willet, Newport.

————

    Number taken, ... **380.**
    Number committed, ... **364.**

STATISTICS.

Privateers' and Captains' Names.	N. of Men	Escap'd.	Died.	Joined Br.Ships	Remain in Prison
Brig Dolton, Captain Johnston, . .	120	21	8	7	84
Sloop Sally, Captain Brown, . . .	52	6	7	16	23
Brig Fancy, Captain Lee, . . .	56	11	2	0	43
Brig Lexington, Captain Johnston, .	51	6	1	26	18
Schooner Warren, Captain Ravel, . .	40	2	0	6	32
PARTS OF CREWS TAKEN, IN PRISON.					
Brig Freedom, **Captain Cluston,** .	11	3	1	0	7
Ship Reprisal, **Captain Weeks,** . .	10	2	0	3	5
Sloop Hawk, ...	6	0	0	0	6
Schooner Hawk, Captain Hibbart, .	6	0	0	0	6
Schooner Black Snake, Captain Lucran,	3	6	0	0	3
Ship Oliver Cromwell, . . .	7	1	0	2	4
Letter of Marque Janey, **Captain Rolls,**	2	1	0	0	1
Brig Cabot, ...	3	0	0	0	3
True Blue, Captain **Furlong,** . .	1	0	0	0	1
Ranger, ...	1	0	0	0	1
Sloop Lucretia, ...	2	0	0	0	2
Musquito Tender, ...	1	0	0	1	0
Schooner, Captain **Burnell,** . .	2	1	0	1	0
Sturdy Beggar, ...	3	1	0	0	2
Revenge, Captain **Cunningham,** . .	3	0	0	0	3
	380	55	19	62	244
From Newburyport, ...	53	14	2	1	36
From Marblehead, ...	50	9	1	0	40
From Boston, ...	8	2	1	2	5
From Salem, ...	28	1	0	1	26
From Portsmouth, ...	8	1	0	1	6
Kittery, Berwick, and Old York, .	34	1	4	0	29
Ipswich, Manchester, and Cape Ann,	13	1	1	1	10
Eastward of Old York, . . .	14	2	1	0	11
England, Ireland and Scotland, .	61	7	2	30	22
Towns South of Boston, . .	76	8	5	16	57
East of Boston, ...	9	1	0	0	8
The remainder, of other nations.					
	354	47	17	52	250